NEW ORLEANS HISTORIC HOTELS

PAUL OSWELL

THE
History
PRESS

Published by The History Press
Charleston, SC 29403
www.historypress.net

Copyright © 2014 by Paul Oswell
All rights reserved

Front cover, clockwise from top left: Soniat House, Le Pavillon, Hotel Monteleone, a milk cart outside La Louisane and the Roosevelt Hotel.
Back cover, clockwise from top left: The storming of the Sazerac at the Roosevelt Hotel, the dining room at the Hotel DeSoto and the courtyard at the W French Quarter.

All photos courtesy of the respective hotels unless otherwise noted.

First published 2014

Manufactured in the United States

ISBN 978.1.62619.687.2

Library of Congress CIP data applied for.

Notice: The information in this book is true and complete to the best of our knowledge. It is offered without guarantee on the part of the author or The History Press. The author and The History Press disclaim all liability in connection with the use of this book.

All rights reserved. No part of this book may be reproduced or transmitted in any form whatsoever without prior written permission from the publisher except in the case of brief quotations embodied in critical articles and reviews.

To John, Marie and David.

CONTENTS

Acknowledgements	9
Introduction	11
1. The Early Hotels of New Orleans	21
2. The St. Charles Hotel	34
3. The New Astor Hotel (Formerly the Cosmopolitan Hotel)	43
4. Maison de Ville	47
5. The Roosevelt (Formerly the Grunewald and the Fairmont)	55
6. Audubon Cottages	64
7. Le Pavillon (Formerly the New Hotel Denechaud and the Hotel DeSoto)	69
8. Omni Royal Orleans (Formerly the City Exchange, the St. Louis Hotel, the Royal Orleans Hotel)	77
9. Soniat House	85
10. The Monteleone	90
11. The Cornstalk Hotel	99
12. The Bourbon Orleans Hotel	103
13. Le Richelieu	109
14. Andrew Jackson French Quarter Hotel	116
15. The Lafitte Guest House	120
16. Place D'Armes Hotel	125
17. Further Historic Hotels: Short Stories	129
18. French Quarter Guest Houses: Lamothe House, Inn on Ursulines, Inn on St. Peter, Inn on St. Ann	146

CONTENTS

19. The Jung and the Rise of Canal Street Hotels	149
20. Hotels in Modern-Day New Orleans	151
Appendix I: Meeting the Official Historian of the Hotel Monteleone	157
Appendix II: Recipes from Selected New Orleans Hotels	161
Appendix III: Historical Guidebook Hotel Directories	167
Appendix IV: New Orleans Historic Hotel Directory	171
Bibliography	173
About the Author	175

ACKNOWLEDGEMENTS

Many thanks to my editors Kirsten Schofield, Julia Turner and Chad Rhoad for their hard work, assistance and patience. Thanks to all at The History Press. Many thanks to Eric, Jennifer and all the staff at the Historic New Orleans Collection Williams Research Center. Special thanks to Marc Becker of the New Orleans Hotel Collection for his support and insider knowledge and to Jenny Adams for her kind help on very short notice. A huge thanks to everyone at each of the hotels who assisted me and, in some cases, fed and sheltered me: Richard Poe II and Cassie Holman, Caitlin Switzer, Pam Sitzman, Janna Holderer, Roberta Grove, Danielle Plauche-Shaw, Amy Valentino, Nikki Ritzenthaler, Betsie Gambel, Jodi LaFranca, Paul Loisel, Megan Uram and Emily Liuzza. Thanks to Kevin O'Mara for suggesting that I might be up to this task in the first place and for taking the author's photo. Thanks to all my New Orleans friends and family for their encouragement, support and for selflessly drinking cocktails in hotel bars with me.

INTRODUCTION

My first visit to New Orleans was in 2001. I'll never forget stepping off that plane at Louis Armstrong Airport after a thirteen-hour journey from London, England—straight into that sweet, sweaty, cloying heat. If you've been here during the summer months, you'll know the heat I mean. I chose to visit in July for some unknown reason. I guess I didn't know any better back then.

The first hotel I stayed in here wasn't particularly historic. In fact, it was undeniably modern: the W New Orleans on Poydras Street. Even as I write, that same hotel is slowly transitioning to become a new hotel—Le Meridien. Yes, it's a change of name within brands owned by the same corporation, but it also neatly reflects the subtle changes that the New Orleans hospitality industry constantly reacts to. These changes have shaped the city's character as well as its physical skyline, and this is the story I wanted to tell here.

Researching this book, I was also fascinated by the fact that the neighborhood surrounding the W Poydras was witness to some of the city's most dramatic developments—events that influenced the complicated political and social history of the Crescent City.

I've now been lucky enough to have been a guest at the majority of the hotels in this beautiful city. Their rooms have witnessed fortuitous successes, glorious failures, love affairs, dramatic break-ups, drunken escapades and long hours of soul searching over room service sandwiches. And that's just when *I've* been staying at them.

INTRODUCTION

Hotels have been an integral part of life in New Orleans since their inception. They have played host to pirates and politicians (no cheap jokes, please), provided a stage for the city's wildest celebrations as well as, in the times of slavery, its most shameful practices.

In the rooms of New Orleans hotels, military campaigns were plotted, treasure was divided, assassination plots were uncovered, great works of literature were inspired, celebrities were courted, tragedies were witnessed and disaster relief efforts were coordinated. Radio stations broadcast from their top floors, great jazz musicians lit up their ballrooms, authors drank way too many cocktails in their bars (and occasionally did some writing) and, in the most extreme of times, official seats of government were even set up within their walls.

Whole lives were led and dramatic deaths took place—and the numerous tours that take place every evening in the French Quarter tell us that we have the ghosts to prove it. For the supernaturally inclined, and for our general amusement since that's how we roll in New Orleans (where we put the *fun* in funeral), I've included any haunted tales in the lagniappe section at the end of each chapter. This is a city, after all, where the real estate notices that hang outside houses sometimes have an extra board attached to the For Sale sign that reads, "Not Haunted."

As for lagniappe, it's a local term that means a little something extra given out to the customer for free. Here you'll find gossip, trivia, ghost stories, celebrity residents and all manner of other frivolous details.

If you're ever in New Orleans, no matter where you're staying, I very much recommend touring (with a cocktail, of course—that's practically obligatory) the Monteleone, the Roosevelt, Le Pavillon or, in fact, any of the hotels mentioned in this book. Slivers of history are there to be seen, and if you're lucky, you might even run into employees who were there at the time. People stay a long time if they have good jobs in honorable places, and in every old hotel I went to, the longtime employees (some there for thirty, forty, fifty years) all said the same thing: "It's like a family here."

They won't need much persuasion to tell you their stories. No doubt there are dozens that remain untold. I hope you enjoy the ones I relate to you here.

Paul Oswell
New Orleans, 2014.

INTRODUCTION

A Note About Addresses in the French Quarter

As I started research on the addresses of some of the older buildings and hotels, I came to a quick conclusion, one that on further reading seemed to be backed up by far more accomplished authors and researchers than myself. Essentially, in the nineteenth century, the address system in New Orleans, and particularly the French Quarter, was—to put it diplomatically—charmingly inconsistent. The standard numbering of houses that we assume now dates back to 1894, so all addresses referred to after that date correspond directly to their modern-day equivalents. I have, where possible, used modern-day addresses when referring to numbered buildings before 1894, but a more useful way of locating buildings was just to name the corners of the streets on which they stood. My apologies for any errant addresses—it wouldn't be New Orleans if the sun didn't rise over the West Bank, street pronunciation wasn't a linguistic guessing game and addresses didn't entail at least a small amount of confusion.

Selected Timeline

1799: Hotel d'Orleans opens, the first recognized hotel in the city.
1824: The Orleans Theatre and Hotel, Beale's Hotel and Le Veau Qui Tête are listed as hotels in the city directory.
1825: Anecdotal evidence that L'Hôtel des Etrangers is operating; reports say that the Marquis de Lafayette stayed there.
1827: The Planter's Hotel on Canal is reported as being open for business.
1832: Bishop's City Hotel opens on the corner of Camp and Common Streets.
1834: L'Hôtel des Etrangers receives Napoleon's former surgeon, Francois Antommarchi.
1835: The original Planter's Hotel on Canal Street collapses, killing ten people, though forty escape with their lives.
1837: The first St. Charles Hotel opens.
1838: The Verandah Hotel opens on the corner of St. Charles Avenue and Common Street. The City Exchange opens with entrances on St. Louis Street and on Royal Street.
1841: Fire destroys the City Exchange.
1842: The City Exchange reopens, though it is now known as the St. Louis Hotel.

INTRODUCTION

1851: Fire destroys the first St. Charles and the Verandah.

1852: The second St. Charles Hotel opens.

1884: The first Hotel Denechaud opens on the corner of Carondelet and Perdido Streets. The St. Louis becomes the Hotel Royal, soon to close down.

1886: Antonio Monteleone buys 54 Royal Street and operates a small hotel from the property.

1892: The Cosmopolitan Hotel opens on Royal Street.

1893: The Hotel Grunewald Opens on Baronne Street.

1894: The second St. Charles Hotel is destroyed by fire.

1895: The third St. Charles Hotel opens.

1898: Antonio Monteleone expands his hotel operations to a five-story townhouse and ownership of the Commercial Hotel on the same block.

1903: The Orleans Hotel, an incarnation of the Hotel D'Orleans, closes as the building is bought by an ice company.

1906: Hotel Bruno opens at 210 Dauphine.

1907–08: The Hotel Monteleone opens as Antonio Monteleone consolidates his properties on Royal Street. The Jung Hotel opens on Canal Street. The New Hotel Denechaud opens on Poydras. The Grunewald expands.

1910: The New Hotel Denechaud becomes the Hotel DeSoto.

1916: The Lafayette Hotel opens at Lafayette Square.

1919: Hotel Bruno is refurbished and becomes the Planter's Hotel.

1923: The Grunewald is remodeled and reopens as the Roosevelt Hotel.

1925: The Jung Hotel expands. The Cosmopolitan Hotel becomes the New Astor Hotel.

1930: The Planter's Hotel becomes known as the Senator.

1960s: A rash of historic buildings in the French Quarter are converted to hotels and "motor hotels," including the Cornstalk, Andrew Jackson Hotel, Hotel Provincial and the Place D'Armes.

1960: The Royal Orleans Hotel opens on the original site of the City Exchange/St. Louis Hotel.

1963: The Hotel DeSoto closes.

1965: The Roosevelt Hotel is sold and becomes the Fairmont Hotel.

1967: The Senator closes.

1969: A moratorium is introduced, dictating that new hotel construction is now prohibited in the French Quarter. The city naturally sees hotel openings in the Central Business District (CBD), on Canal Street and in the Warehouse District.

1971: The Hotel DeSoto reopens as Le Pavillon; the New Astor Hotel has closed.

INTRODUCTION

1974: The third St. Charles Hotel closes, and the building is demolished.

1980s–1990s: Thanks to an exodus of middle-class families from downtown New Orleans, a large number of downtown department stores close. Many of these buildings are converted into hotels for the growing tourism and convention industry.

1984: Soniat House opens as a hotel.

Late 1990s–2000s: Hotel capacity in the city reaches thirty-seven thousand rooms, catering to some ten million annual tourists. Historic buildings open as hotels, including the Ritz Carlton.

2005: Hurricane Katrina hits, followed by the failure of the federal levee system, causing widespread, citywide damage. The Jung Hotel closes. The Fairmont Hotel closes for refurbishment, as do the Hyatt Regency and the Ritz-Carlton.

2009: The Fairmont Hotel reopens as, once again, the Roosevelt Hotel.

2011: The Hyatt Regency reopens. The Hotel Modern opens at Lee Circle.

2012: The Hyatt French Quarter opens.

New Orleans: Times, People and Places

I realize that not everyone who might read this book will be from New Orleans, and even if they are, they might not necessarily be a history buff. I've tried to avoid telling the same stories more than once, a more difficult task than it sounds given that almost all the hotels in this book existed at the same time, and were witness to the same citywide events and, in some cases, were even frequented by the same historical figures.

So that I don't have to give the same backstory or historical context every time I mention a person or event, I thought it a good idea to give a very general introduction to some of the recurring historical themes and people—a cast of characters, if you will.

If you're a New Orleans resident or visitor or scholar, then feel free to skip this part, since you're probably familiar with the people and events. If you're unaware that, for example, America had a Civil War in 1861, then I'd advise at least a quick glance at these introductions, just so things make more sense.

INTRODUCTION

Times

American Civil War (1861–65)
At the time of the Civil War, New Orleans was the largest city in the Southern states. It was a major target for the Union army, and its soldiers occupied the city for much of the conflict. The city was captured in 1862 without a battle in the city itself, meaning it was spared widespread destruction. General Butler (nicknamed the "Beast" due the severity of his rule) subjected the city to martial law and Federal troops continued to occupy the city even beyond the end of hostilities. The war brought hard times to a city so reliant, even in that period, on tourist revenue, and many hotels were taken over to become boardinghouses for soldiers or military hospitals.

Reconstruction (1866–67)
This refers to both the political reconstruction of the Southern states, restoring them to the Union, and the material reconstruction of New Orleans, where hotels—having undergone the refurbishments needed to once again welcome visitors—resumed as normal a life as they could. Many were still having to house returning Confederate soldiers at this time and, as a result, not earning much in the way of revenue. It was a hard time for many hotels in the city, as well as the local economy in general.

Storyville (1897–1917)
In 1897, a program of social reform was implemented by Alderman Sidney Story in an effort to contain prostitution and disease in New Orleans. Bound by the streets of Basin, North Robertson, Iberville and St. Louis, this sixteen-block area signified a place where prostitution, while not legal, was certainly decriminalized. It was officially known as the District but, much to the Alderman's chagrin, became colloquially known as Storyville. The houses ranged from cheap flophouses to upscale bordellos, and with it came a multitude of characters and miscreants. Famously, the *Blue Books* were published (essentially directories for the brothels and individual prostitutes in Storyville), and it was here that jazz music flourished amid a hotbed of debauched practices. In 1917, prostitution was made fully illegal, the U.S. Navy not wanting distractions (or disease) to weigh on its sailors.

Hurricane Katrina (2005)
On August 29, 2005, a devastating tropical cyclone named Hurricane Katrina made landfall on the Gulf Coast between Florida and Texas. It bought

INTRODUCTION

widespread flooding and destruction, and in New Orleans, it caused a failure of the federal levee system, the largest man-made disaster in the history of the United States. Large areas of the city flooded, and in Louisiana alone over 1,500 deaths were reported. The effects were long lasting, with entire neighborhoods wiped out, massive amounts of the population displaced and many businesses closing completely. Some eventually reopened (the Roosevelt Hotel), and some didn't (the Jung Hotel).

People

Jean Lafitte (1776–1823)
The most notorious pirate of his day in New Orleans, though he probably preferred the term *privateer*. He and his brother, Pierre, operated a distribution business in the city to fence their ill-gotten gains. Although the base of their operations was an island in Barataria Bay, Louisiana, the Lafittes spent a substantial amount of time in the city and even assisted General Jackson in his victory against the British in 1815. Several local businesses pay homage to him, notably Lafitte's Blacksmith Shop (one of the oldest bars in the United States) and Lafitte's Guesthouse, which face each other across the corner of Bourbon and St. Philip Streets.

Andrew Jackson (1767–1845)
The man who would become the seventh president of the United States was also one of New Orleans's greatest heroes. Having covered himself in glory during the battle against the British in 1812, he went on to show even more fortitude and tactical bravery in the 1815 Battle of New Orleans, taking his 5,000 troops to victory over the 7,500 soldiers of the British army, only losing 13 soldiers in the process. A constitutional controversy arose as he declared martial law in the city, arresting a federal judge in the process, but Jackson relented, was declared a hero and went on to become president in 1829.

John James Audubon (1785–1851)
Born in Haiti, Audubon immigrated to the United States and became one of the country's best-known ornithologists, naturalists and painters. His illustrated book *Birds of America* is still considered one of the finest works on bird life ever completed. He arrived in New Orleans in 1821 and spent a substantial portion of the next fifteen years or so in and around Louisiana. His accommodations, some of which are now hotel rooms, are well documented.

INTRODUCTION

Lafcadio Hearn (1850–1904)
Hearn was a Greek-born writer who traveled extensively overseas, particularly in Japan. He also traveled in the United States and, in 1877, arrived in New Orleans, where he filed regular dispatches for a newspaper in Cincinnati. He stayed on and lived in New Orleans for nearly ten years, writing for local publications such as the *Daily City Item* and the *Times Democrat*. His writing was especially insightful and evocative, and his essays (he was also incredibly prolific) remain some of the most interesting and descriptive renderings of New Orleans life at the time. He moved on to the West Indies in 1887.

Huey P. Long (1895–1935)
Governor of Louisiana from 1928 to 1932 and U.S. senator from 1932 to 1935, Long was a gregarious, outspoken populist who rallied vigorously against the rich and the banks, selling himself as a true man of the people. His motto "Every Man a King" and his everyman lifestyle led to him being referred to as the "Kingfish," and he was as divisive as he was outrageous. He was a famous manipulator of the media in New Orleans and set up his political headquarters in the Roosevelt Hotel. He was assassinated in Baton Rouge in 1935.

Places

The story of the development and civic planning of New Orleans would, and does, fill up many books on its own. If you want a full, detailed and hugely interesting picture, I recommend *Bienville's Dilemma* by Richard Campanella. Just to give context to some of the neighborhoods mentioned in these accounts, here is a very bare-bones synopsis:

The city was founded by the French in 1718 due to its location near the juncture of the Mississippi River and the Gulf of Mexico. In 1762, the French gave Louisiana to the Spanish. The French Quarter (the First Municipality) was developed on a grid by the river, but thanks to a huge fire in 1788, most of the architectural styles you see today are Spanish.

In 1801, Louisiana ceded back to the French, and within two years, Napoleon sold it to the United States. The French Quarter was largely Europeans and Creoles (people of mixed Hispanic, Caribbean, African and European race), and the Americans who arrived to live here populated what was known as the American Sector (also known as the Second Municipality, which became the modern-day Central Business District) across Canal Street.

INTRODUCTION

The Garden District (uptown) was laid out in 1832 to house new American residents who wanted to avoid the Creoles and Europeans. Land developers in the nineteenth century branched out across Esplanade Avenue to make neighborhoods in what became the Marigny and the Bywater (the Third Municipality). Free people of color—those of African descent who were not enslaved—became skilled craftspeople and musicians and lived in what is now the Tremé, north of the French Quarter.

By 1900, the city was more or less taking on its modern shape, with the renumbering of the French Quarter taking place just before the turn of the twentieth century.

1.
THE EARLY HOTELS OF NEW ORLEANS

Hotel life in New Orleans then was something sui generis. There was a dash of excitement and Bohemianism about it that made it [e]specially attractive. The social life of that period was very gay, and the hotels were the centres of all this gaiety.
—*Lafcadio Hearn, 1885*

Eighty years after the founding of the city of La Nouvelle-Orléans in 1718 by Jean-Baptiste Le Moyne de Bienville, the city's first recorded hotel opened for business in the grit and grime of the French Quarter. After what must have been an exhausting few minutes of trying to think what to call it, it was named (and please try to conceal your astonishment) the Hotel d'Orleans, and it received its first guests in 1799. This opening was fortuitously timed, coinciding very nicely with the opening of the newly rebuilt Cabildo, which had been erected to be the seat of the Spanish municipal government.

The Hotel d'Orleans was built at 541 Chartres Street by Samuel Moore, a prominent property owner in the city at that time. Little is documented about its early days as a business, though incredibly, it lasted in one form or another until 1906, when it was bought by the Cosmopolitan Ice Company. The *Daily News* of the day had this to say about the hotel: "The Orleans Hotel was, in the palmy days of the 1850's, the favorite rendezvous of the rich planters who came on frequent visits of pleasure and business, principally during the French Opera season and about the time that sugar grinding was over, and there was money to spend as freely as one could wish."

A milk cart pauses outside La Louisiane Hotel, 1903. *Detroit Publishing Company.*

At the turn of the nineteenth century, those palmy days had not yet arrived, and the building was likely not much more than a glorified boardinghouse, just somewhere for travelers to sleep that would perhaps provide some meager meals and provisions. The days of full service, minibars and concierges were yet to be even imagined; for now, a room to oneself and sitting down to a meal in a dining room that was only a minor den of iniquity was considered an embarrassment of luxurious riches.

Previous to the relative splendor of the Hotel d'Orleans and the hotels that would soon follow it, most transients and visitors had been accommodated either in private houses or in small-scale rooming houses. These places were literally nothing to write home about, and even anecdotal evidence is scarce. There was one of note, however, though it wasn't always remembered for the best reasons. It was called Tremoulet's, after its owner, Bernard Tremoulet, and it had a particularly memorable landlady in the shape of his domineering wife.

The architect Benjamin Henry Latrobe, who built the New Orleans Custom House in 1807, was one early visitor to Tremoulet's (located at the corner of St. Peter Street and Rue de La Levée, now Decatur Street). He recalled it somewhat joylessly as "a large boarding house," and he had a couple of choice memories to share in his 1876 book, *The Journal of Latrobe*: "Madame Tremoulet—why should I conceal the name of such a termagant—is one of those notorious for her cruelty. She is a small, mild-faced creature who weeps over the absence of her daughter."

Latrobe goes on to relate the story of how Madame Tremoulet had, in his educated opinion, one of the most wonderful servants in town. After the servant failed at a near-impossible task, which she had been set by La Tremoulet, Latrobe tells how the mistress of the house stripped her in public, tied her to a bed post and whipped her with a cow skin until she bled. Nothing like a public beating to put your house guests at ease, after all, but then what would you expect from such a complete termagant? (I had to look it up, too: it's a turbulent, harsh-tempered woman).

NEW ORLEANS HISTORIC HOTELS

Many of the first hotels in New Orleans grew up around already popular eating and drinking spots. Although its original construction date is unclear, by 1808, the Café des Réfugiés was doing a brisk trade with the local population of ne'er-do-wells at 514 St. Philip Street under the management of a man called John-Baptiste Thiot. Thiot was particularly known for his strong alcoholic concoctions made from, among other things, a powerful, raw form of tequila.

In his 2010 essay, *New Orleans Nostalgia*, Ned Hémard takes up the story: "In 1833, Pierre Hurtubise, Jr., sold the building with its peculiar patio to Jean Louis Arnaud for $16,100. This forced Thiot to relocate the Café des Réfugiés to a building in the 900 block of Decatur Street opposite the French Market."

A view of Exchange Alley, lined with small boardinghouses and hotels, taken in 1900. *Detroit Publishing Company.*

According to Stanley Arthur in his book *Old New Orleans*, the Café des Réfugiés was a hotbed of characters: "[It was] frequented in the very old days by fugitives from the islands of the Antilles and located at 287 Old Levee [now 921 Decatur street]. This structure had been previously occupied by R. Revel's Le Veau qui Tête (the Suckling Calf) tavern, doing business there from 1821–1825 at what was then 58 rue de La Levée (Old Levee Street)."

It was on this block on Decatur that the Hôtel de la Marine opened, neighboring the Café des Réfugiés. We know that in 1809, the hotel was owned by Jean Noël Déstréhan and was apparently leased to none other than our old friend Bernard Tremoulet, flush with success from his termagant-run boardinghouse, which was itself later upgraded to the more grandly named Tremoulet House Hotel.

Hémard also reports that the Hôtel de la Marine was frequented by none other than the city's own beloved local pirates, the Lafitte brothers, Jean and

Pierre. To have local business owners tell it, there wasn't an establishment that these lovable rogues *didn't* spend time in, but pirates do admittedly need to vary their venues for plotting, cackling and dividing up booty. In any case, Hémard postulates that the hotel was a popular rendezvous for "the strange, adventurous and eclectic mix of characters that frequented the city's Riverfront." At least in this regard of the makeup of the city's characters, the more things change, the more they stay the same.

It didn't take long for the choice of accommodations being offered to the discerning traveler to expand. The 1824 New Orleans City Directory has Jean (aka John) Davis as the proprietor of the "Orleans Theatre, Ballroom and Hotel," though this is a different venture from the Hotel d'Orleans. This concern was located on Orleans Avenue and is now the Bourbon Orleans Hotel, which has its own fascinating story and receives a more detailed history later on in this book.

There are two other hotels listed in the 1824 directory. One is a place called Beales Hotel, located on Canal Street, though the book *New Orleans Architecture: Jefferson City* by Friends of the Cabildo has the same hotel located on Chartres Street. This was perhaps a different property run by the same family (and hence given the same name).

The account talks of Thomas Beale Jr., an "upright and economical" young man who "ran the family hotel on Chartres Street very industriously, saw that it was finely furnished and offered excellent meals." He apparently even bought an uptown plantation to cultivate vegetable and pasture stock for use in the hotel kitchen. Sustainability was the norm in those days, and no doubt the hotel would in this modern age win awards for its farm-to-table approach and corporate social responsibility. That said, the actual cultivation was probably undertaken by slaves, so perhaps not.

In any case, the Friends of the Cabildo had more to report about this upright gentleman: "[In 1820], Thomas Jr. was left to carry on the family business alone. He did this quite well, soon moving from Chartres Street to larger quarters at The Planter's and the Merchant's Hotel on Canal Street."

The other listed hotel is the aforementioned Hotel Le Veau Qui Tête, run and owned by a Mr. Pierre Giraudeau. The Suckling Calf was a place of fine culinary practices and one that was held in some high esteem according to John Kendall in his 1922 *History of New Orleans*:

> At the corner of St. Peter Street still stands a building which, in the early part of the nineteenth century, was famous as a hotel and restaurant under the name of "Le Veau Qui Tête." To the same epoch belonged the Hotel

de la Marine, which stood in the vicinity of the French Market, near St. Philip Street. These were, however, small establishments, though sufficient for the accommodation of the travelers who passed through the city in that primitive day.

Bliss it must have been in that primitive day to be alive, but to be a guest at a basic guesthouse in New Orleans was presumably very heaven.

Another early hotel, L'Hôtel des Etrangers, receives a mention, albeit a nondescript one, in the 1895 book *New Orleans as It Was* by Henry C. Castellanos. It is referred to in the account of the landing in New Orleans of none other than the surgeon to Napoleon Bonaparte himself, Dr François Antommarchi.

The year was 1834, and Castellanos relates: "[He] was escorted to Salle Davis on Orleans Street…[and] was provisionally lodged at Marti's Hotel, known today as L'Hôtel des Etrangers on Chartres Street, below St. Louis, where a continuous levee was held, an increasing stream of struggling humanity, and, at night, a serenade given him by the artists of the French Theatre."

There isn't much written evidence outside this report to confirm when or exactly where Marti's Hotel operated, or of when it became L'Hôtel des Etrangers. We can just assume that the hotel was somewhere on this stretch of Chartres below St. Louis and that—as Castallenos's account goes on to explain—it was impressive enough to move Antommarchi to exclaim that he intended to make New Orleans his permanent home (see Chapter 3).

One later record we have of the "Strangers Hotel" (its name had since become Anglicized) is from local newspaper the *Picayune* of November 1860: "[It was] one of those quaint old French public houses where one found at very reasonable charges the comfort of a home circle; delicacies of the French table; convivial pleasures of the first-rate boarding houses, combined with the entire freedom precious to those who preferred hotel life to all others."

By 1832, a hotel called Bishop's City Hotel had also sprung up on the corner of Camp and Common Streets. There are few stories about this property, but the facts seem to be that it was built by Karl Frederick Zimpel, the famous surveyor who is responsible for one of the most reputable early topographical surveys of New Orleans.

An 1842 engraved illustration by John V. Childs in the city directory shows the building, listed as "City Hotel, late Bishop's," suggesting that it had already changed its name. The hotel doesn't come across as a place of great leisure pursuits or revelry, the only paragraph in the directory attesting to the "superintending care of Madame Shall, especially her care to those

NEW ORLEANS HISTORIC HOTELS

A postcard of the old St. Louis Hotel, with a view from Royal Street, from 1907. *C.B. Mason.*

suffering from yellow fever during time periods of epidemic." Let the good times roll, indeed.

By 1853, it had moved beyond the care of the infirm and was serving some of the best food in the city according to the *Times-Picayune*, which, in 1840 reported somewhat breathlessly (and exhaustively):

> *The art of dining was at a point as near perfection here as anywhere in the world. The menu for a dinner for twelve* [at the City Hotel] *was turtle soup, sheepshead, redfish, buffalo tongue, ham glaces, filets of duck, green peas, asparagus, turkey stuffed with truffles, Perigaud sauce, saddle of lamb, beef tenderloin, filets of chicken, cotelietes of squabs, croustade of snipe, saddle of venison, canvas back, mallard and teal duck, etc."*

If this near-endless conveyor of exotic meats proved too much, or if you didn't have four hours to spend eating a single meal, there was also a ten-cent menu that just covered the basics: "Teal duck pie, oyster pie, oxtail soup, hashed beef and potatoes, roast beef, bread, butter, pickles and a glass of lemonade." For diners on the go, it was the obvious choice.

The land is now covered by a small corner of the large, modern Sheraton New Orleans Hotel that occupies the entire block. Yellow fever victims would likely be given short shrift if they came in looking for any superintending care these days. At least now there's a Starbucks, though, so skinny soy lattes are no problem at all.

By the mid-1830s, work was being started on the more opulent "Exchange Hotels" that would soon spring up around the Canal Street divide of the First and Second Municipalities. Notably, these included the City Exchange (in the Creole First Municipality) and the St. Charles Hotel (in the Anglo Second Municipality). These larger, much more ornate properties were there to seduce the local titans of industry, with a view to taking their money from them, of course.

In a game-changing development, the new exchange hotels offered food, accommodation, banking and conference space all in one place ("commerce" and "exchange" were often, of course, period euphemisms for the slave trade). They were the first places to invest any kind of money in interior decoration that wasn't merely functional and employed great artists of the day to design and decorate their public spaces.

We will look at one of the biggest ones, the St. Charles Hotel, in more detail, but let's note here that its construction spurred a flurry of new hotels. The City Exchange—also the subject of its own chapter as the Omni Royal New Orleans (Chapter 8)—was an almost direct riposte to the St. Charles. Another such hotel was the Verandah, which was constructed diagonally across from the St. Charles on the corner of St. Charles Avenue and Common Street at a cost of around $300,000.

The Verandah came about as a result of some unfriendly competition between Richard B. Pritchard, who was an Englishman, and Thomas Barrett, who was an Irishman. The two were both early members of the cartel that sought to build the St. Charles Hotel, but (and try to conceal your surprise here) they argued relentlessly over their homeland politics. Their associates begged them to put their differences behind them, to forget Old World arguments to pursue this particularly New World dream. Pritchard utterly refused, storming out of a meeting with the ominous threat, "I will build a hotel of my own."

He did. The Verandah opened soon after its neighbor in May 1838, getting its name from—shockingly—the grand outside balcony or, if you will, verandah that loomed over the sidewalk. This addition gave views to the guests and either shade or shelter to anyone who cared to stand underneath it.

This wasn't even the biggest selling point of the hotel, though. That would be its grand dining room, which boasted elaborate frescos and fine statues, the former of which were created by an artist called Canova, a nephew of one of the era's celebrated sculptors.

Peer-review websites were, of course, the stuff of a madman's dreams, but luckily we have the published diaries of affluent travelers (surely the travel blogs of the day) to give us some insight as to how these establishments operated. Lady Emmeline Stuart Wortley, an English poet and writer, stayed at the Verandah in 1849 and wrote about it in a book which documents her travels in the United States between 1849 and 1850, a book which bears the unswervingly literal title of *Travels Within the United States During 1849 and 1850.*

Here's what Lady Wortley had to report: "We are at a very splendid and comfortable hotel called The Verandah. It reminds me of a Parisian one. The St. Charles is the largest of all the hotels in New Orleans but it is much crowded, and we were recommended to try this, as it is quieter, and thus pleasanter for the ladies."

Lady W. goes on to praise the St. Charles at some length, implying that she actually would rather be staying there, then damns the Verandah with faint praise and ends with a complaint about the price: "The attendance at [this hotel] is admirable, and all the arrangements excellent. But the charges are much higher than usual in the States."

She then relates a rather tedious story about being harassed by "a little Swede" at dinner (someone from Sweden, not the root vegetable). In any case, she is by and large quite impressed by the place, especially the "airy apartments" as they saved her from "an early termination from these frying-pan temperatures." She was being dramatic then, of course, but her early termination sadly did come just five years later, when she died of dysentery while traveling in the Ottoman Empire, a case of out of the frying pan and onto the pyre.

The Verandah was eventually subsumed into the same management as the St. Charles Hotel, and, as befell many a building in those days, it perished in a fire in 1850, one in which the St. Charles was also destroyed. The latter was rebuilt, but the Verandah did not enjoy a similar resurrection, though it did eventually become a hotel again some one hundred years later (see the lagniappe section at the end of this chapter).

By the mid-1830s, the emergence of train travel was also dictating commerce. The construction of a depot for the New Orleans and Carrollton Railroad was completed in 1835, and a hotel—the Carrollton Hotel—was also built, railway hotels being an international phenomenon by this time. Reports of the time call it a "fashionable resort" and a "plantation-like building."

The Carrollton Hotel set its sights on attracting an upper-class clientele and offered various sporting pursuits among its amenities, which included a shooting gallery, a bowling green (a very British addition and a rarity in the

United States) and a tenpin bowling alley. A poplar racetrack (the Eclipse) was only a few minutes away if guests felt like a sporting bet.

The *Times-Picayune* of June 1840 reported from the scene soon after the opening, describing the curious gaming stations:

> Sunday excursion trains carried hundreds of passengers to the Carrollton House…the dining room opened upon the first gallery…upon the upper gallery, the ladies assembled. The galleries ran all around the house and on the side…a little game was played with hooks and a ring. In the garden flourished every kind of bud, blade, tint and odor. On the rear gallery was a square box covered with a variety of holes into which players pitched copper quoits, about the circumference of an English penny.

The hotel and its grounds became a civilized weekend escape for affluent city dwellers, a "rural community" according to the history provided by the *Transit Reader's Digest* of 1968. It embellishes this idyll even more: "The fountains sent forth bizarre and conical jets of cool, limpid water, and the sweet songsters of nature makes the groves resound with their silvery voices. Hundreds, nay, thousand flock thither every Sunday."

The original hotel burned down in 1842 (a seemingly compulsory rights of passage for hotels in this period) but was rebuilt by the following year, though it eventually fell into disrepair and was demolished.

There were several examples of restaurants that developed into hotels, one assumes simply by opening up a small number of rooms to overnight guests, much as the Hotel d'Orleans and Le Veau Qui Tête had done a century earlier. In 1903, even Antoine's Restaurant was taking in guests, such was the demand and easy money to be made.

Other restaurants also opened their own separate accommodations. The 1903 city directory lists a Hotel Bero at 226 Bourbon Street. This was run by Mrs. Victor Bero, who was also the proprietor of the popular Victor's Restaurant at 211 Bourbon Street. A 1903 American Medical Association journal recommends the place as somewhere to stay in the same breath as many of the larger, more famous places, so it must have been doing something right. The Beros also owned the Hotel Chalmette, which stood at 100 St. Charles Avenue and opened in 1881.

Fabacher's Restaurant, run by the Fabacher brothers (Albert, John, Louis, Jacob, Peter and Lawrence), was also branching out by adding rooms. Situated at 137 Royal Street, the place was essentially a German beer hall, or *rathskeller*. Predictably, there are no affluent travel journals telling of stays

A street view looking toward Jung Hotel building, 1931. *Photo by Mr. Benton Hickok for National Weather Service, NOAA's America's Coastlines Collection.*

there, but a 1911 *Kappa Alpha Journal* describes Fabacher's bohemian restaurants as "being known to 'theatrical' people throughout the country" and the rathskeller as "being conservative and quietly elaborate."

Peter was a German immigrant with a brewing background. This expertise ran in the family and his brother, Lawrence Fabacher, founded the Jackson Brewing Co., best known for producing Jax Beer.

As trade and professional associations began to frequent New Orleans, their directories are often the only records of some of the smaller hotels, which seemed to come and go without much of a legacy. From these, we can ascertain that a hotel by the name of Penn's Hotel was at the corner of St. Charles and Poydras Street from at least 1899 to 1914. The Commercial Hotel and the Hotel Metropole were apparently a similar breed. In 1899, they were also listed with Penn's as options for visiting dentists, priced at fifty cents to a dollar per night, a market being fought over by apparently dozens of small, owner-operated guesthouses.

Similar properties existed across the downtown area and have since disappeared into obscurity: the Milan Hotel, the Balize, the Burke Hotel, Osborne Hotel, Richardson's Hotel on Conti Street, the Park View Hotel on Camp Street and others. The Hotel de Louisiane, which was at 717 Customhouse Street (the old Zacharie mansion), has at least a few details about it included in a vintage print advertisement: "50 rooms. Celebrated for its fine French and Creole cuisine. European plan: Rooms 50 cents and up, bath included."

NEW ORLEANS HISTORIC HOTELS

Fragments pop up in old newspaper clippings: The Mansion House Hotel on New Levee Street that held masked balls but would not admit people to the barroom with weapons "of any kind"; the Marigny Hotel on Victory Street (now Decatur Street in the Marigny); the Mexican Hotel, the address of which is unclear though it existed as early as 1819 and may or may not have been the same as the Mexican Gulf Hotel that was in business in 1895. In 1886, a business called the Southern Hotel stood at the corner of Julia and Carondelet Streets. The *Weekly States* reported its burning down, causing the death of Louis Kessner, who—fun fact—was the flautist for the Grand Opera House.

Despite the odd hotel popping up in uptown neighborhoods, by 1904, the streetcar map lists the "Hotel District" as St. Charles and Common Streets. There is a large concentration in what is now the Central Business District, and even the few hotels in the French Quarter congregated very much toward the Canal Street end, a trend that continues to this day.

If the dizzying pace of New Orleans's hotel development at this point in time is getting too much to keep track of, Mr. Kendall provides us with a very helpful and succinct description of the major hotel players in New Orleans as we nose optimistically into the twentieth century, when tourism picked up speed and the city's hotels started to multiply even further to accommodate the sheer number of visitors:

> *The Hotel Grunewald was established on Baronne Street, near Canal, in 1893. The present magnificent structure, extending back through the square to University Place, dates from 1908. The DeSoto was opened in the spring of 1906. It is a magnificent building covering an entire square on Baronne and Poydras streets.*
>
> *The Monteleone was established in 1901, on Royal Street, one block below Canal Street. The Lafayette occupies a commanding location overlooking Lafayette Square. It was opened to the public in October, 1916. The Planters' Hotel, formerly known as the Hotel Bruno, is situated on Dauphine Street, at the corner of Iberville. It was opened in 1906, and the building was renovated and refurnished in 1919.*

Lafcadio Hearn also gives us a useful overview in even more general terms:

> *The First district boasted of few permanent residents, and its population was largely a floating one. People came to the city as to a new El Dorado to spend six months of the year, make as much money as possible, and then fly North or to Europe for a long summer's holiday.*

NEW ORLEANS HISTORIC HOTELS

A postcard of the grottos and caverns in the Cave, in the Hotel Grunewald, 1915. *Detroit Publishing Company.*

> *The greater portion of the population slept at the hotels or boarding-houses, and dined next morning at some of the thousand restaurants that New Orleans then contained. Day boarders at the hotels were of course numerous, and several hundred outsiders sat down at the tables of the St. Charles every day.*

It was these old institutions, at least now resembling modern hotels and beginning to offer the kinds of services that we recognize today, that laid the foundations of New Orleans's modern-day hospitality industry. Some of these places even survived and continue to welcome guests to a city that can be as beguiling now as it was to dear Lafcadio Hearn.

LAGNIAPPE

The site of the Hotel d'Orleans, 541 Chartres (on the corner of Chartres and Toulouse Streets), is now a branch of Regions Bank.

In the early marketing and advertisements, most hotels provided two price quotes, the European plan and the American plan. Simply put, the

European plan is a quote for lodging only while the American plan included two or three meals a day.

Hotel Bruno was named in honor of Pickwick Club member Bruno Schlegel. By the 1920s and then known as the Planter's Hotel, it was especially popular among vaudeville performers. The hotel was renamed the Senator during the 1930s, when Senator Huey P. Long was especially popular. The Senator closed in May 1967 and became a warehouse for the DH Holmes department store until it was destroyed by fire in 1968. (The building subsequently became the Chateau Sonesta and is now the Hyatt French Quarter).

The DH Holmes department store was made famous in the opening scenes of the novel *A Confederacy of Dunces* by John Kennedy Toole. A bronze statue of its protagonist, Ignatius J. Reilly, sits outside the Canal Street entrance to the Hyatt French Quarter.

As an eighteen-year-old, Lee Harvey Oswald lived with his mother in the Senator Hotel for a short time.

By 1855, the site that had been the Verandah Hotel had been bought and built on by the LW Lyons clothing company, though by the 1950s, the building was once again a hotel—the John Mitchell Hotel, which housed radio station WJBW. The site's legacy of hospitality lives on, and the building is now the Marriott Courtyard New Orleans Downtown.

When the Verandah Hotel burned down in 1855, many newspapers at the time were excited as they had the chance to report on the operation of the city's first ever steam fire engine, nicknamed the "Masheen [*sic*]." Its first assignment did not go well as it needed several repairs before it could even leave the station, and then tragicomic incompetence in its usage was displayed, according to the reports of the day.

2.
THE ST. CHARLES HOTEL

Set the St. Charles down in St. Petersburg and you would think it a palace; in Boston, and ten to one you would christen it a college; in London, and it would marvelously remind you of an exchange; in New Orleans, it is all three.
—*Oakey Hall, 1840*

The abstract concept of New Orleans may be one that evokes many things, but the visualization of a particular building isn't necessarily one of them. St. Louis Cathedral comes close to being representative, or even the Superdome in modern times, but there's no Empire State Building or White House that looms large in the general consciousness.

This wasn't always the case, though, and for a long time, the St. Charles Hotel was the iconographic edifice that conjured up the spirit of New Orleans—or, at least, the new American Sector. It embodied the city in many ways, reflected its shifting fortunes and—having come back from tragedy at least twice—was a near-distillation of the civic resilience of New Orleans's people.

The St. Charles, together with the City Exchange (which became the St. Louis), came into existence thanks at least in part to the sense of rivalry that was growing in a divided city in the early nineteenth century. The first building of any real note to be constructed above Canal Street, it sent a bold message to the largely Creole Vieux Carré—that the Fauborg St. Marie (known as the Second Municipality as well as the American Sector) was where the future of the Crescent City really lay.

A period engraving of the first St. Charles Hotel, 1837. *Via Pelican Publishing Company.*

The French Quarter, as we'll see in the history of the City Exchange (in Chapter 8), didn't take this lying down and soon responded, the sense of competition benefitting the city in many ways.

Several local banking companies existed at this time, and the city was a blank canvas for large-scale investment and speculation. A group named the Exchange Bank was responsible for gathering money enough to embark on a project as big as the construction of the first St. Charles Hotel, the cost at the time projected to be in the arena of $800,000, a phenomenal amount of money in those days.

A potentially iconic building, of course, requires skilled and prestigious architects, and the company of Dakin and Gallier was called in, a pairing having made its mark in the building of, for example, city hall, the French Opera House of New Orleans and the state capitol in Baton Rouge. Construction started in 1835, and within a couple of years, the spectacular cupola sat majestically looking over the former wilderness of the American Sector.

The grand building opened on February 22, 1837, timed to coincide with the birthday of George Washington. A grand ball celebrated this milestone achievement in the progress of New Orleans, and the St. Charles's reputation didn't take long to spread. Although the original management was almost immediately spotted as a mistake, it was quickly replaced with a steady set of hands, and under the auspices of the entertainingly named Mudge and Watrous, the hotel embarked on a phenomenally successful early period.

The hotel left an indelible mark on visitors to the city. The famous quote at the beginning of this chapter from the 1840s is from the American politician, lawyer and writer Oakey Hall. Hall was no slack-jawed hayseed being overwhelmed by the scale of one building—he became mayor of New York and was a particularly well-traveled and educated gentleman. His reaction reflects just how flush these times really were in New Orleans, the city having many amenities that not even the hotbed of culture and progress that was Manhattan had come into yet.

James Silk Buckingham, in his 1842 book, *The Slave States of America*, calls the St. Charles, "Undoubtedly the largest, handsomest and most impressive hotel in the world."

Lafcadio Hearn adds to the sense of awe that surrounded the property, also referencing New York:

> *The new hotel created quite a sensation throughout the country, and New Orleans was given the credit of being the most enterprising—it was already recognized as the most aristocratic city in the United States. It must be remembered that this was before the Americans had become a hotel-building people. There were no Palmer Houses in those days, no Pacific Hotels, and visitors to our shores had to content themselves with the most ordinary of old fashioned inns. The St. Charles was the first of the great hotels of the United States and it was some time before it found a rival in the Astor House of New York.*

The first St. Charles hotel came to a dramatic demise. In January 1851, the hotel was full to the brim, the property riding high with its most prosperous season and housing some eight hundred guests, many of whom were in the building at 11:00 p.m. that night. So successful and crowded was the St. Charles at that time, in fact, that it had sent guests over to its rival, the St. Louis, to cope with the overflow.

It was at this time that the upper part of the hotel was discovered to be on fire. Investigations later would suggest a defective chimney or careless workmen. Nevertheless, the flames raged, and while—miraculously—the guests were evacuated without casualty, the late alerting of and general incompetence of the fire service meant that the damage was much more severe than it might otherwise have been.

NEW ORLEANS HISTORIC HOTELS

A stereoscope looking up the 100 block of St. Charles Avenue toward the second St. Charles Hotel. In it, two streetcars are depicted heading uptown, 1901. *Robert N. Dennis collection of stereoscopic views.*

The fire, according to Hearn, "lit up the entire city" and spread to neighboring blocks, destroying churches, houses and public buildings. In the cold light of day, the damage done totaled around $1 million. (Hearn notes that the hotel itself was only insured for just over $100,000.)

This didn't deter an immediate plan of action, presumably spurred on by the huge financial investments that had been made, not to mention the blow to the image that the American Sector was attempting to project. It's hard to lord it over anyone from the ashes, after all. Within days, the decision to rebuild had been ratified by the St. Charles Company. The project took around twelve months to complete, and in 1852, the second St. Charles Hotel stood on the same spot. The new model was erected much in the same style as the original, though its most distinctive feature—the domed copula—was this time not re-created.

In the late 1850s, the hotel was still providing a suitably sophisticated place for high society to congregate and indulge its urbane lifestyle, replete with its own routines. In her 1860 book, *Wayside Glimpses*, Lillian Foster describes the heady lives of the ladies who lunched in the mid-nineteenth century. Status anxiety was seemingly just as prevalent then as now: "At dinner, served in the early afternoon in the lady's ordinary to which only husbands were admitted," she says, "is revealed the ambition, the ostentation, the panting struggle for superiority in mere external experience, which is the essence of the life of a fashionable woman."

Dinner. Coffee. Siesta. Dress for the opera. Opera. Ball. For ladies "as elegantly gowned" as those in Paris, life was a relentless treadmill of luxury, hence all that panting, presumably. It was, however, not to last much longer—at least, not in New Orleans.

The next decade was to be rife with political upheaval. The hotel was once again running as an extremely profitable business; however, the ogre of the Civil War was lumbering disconcertingly into view, and the hotel would have a front row seat. Over the coming years, many of the campaigns and planning meetings would take place within the walls of the St. Charles.

That the manager at the time, Mr. Hildreth, was a Northerner yet a member of the Confederate Guard was cause for some sticky moments. In May 1862, General Butler sent word that he and his Confederate troops were to arrive in the city and were to take up accommodations in the hotel. Mr. Hildreth refused them entry, saying that the hotel was no longer in business, and a skirmish broke out on the streets leading to several arrests.

Butler and his men broke into the hotel bar and then eventually took control of the entire building, opening it up as a boardinghouse for officers and friends, a position that it kept for the whole of the war. Tourism of any kind was understandably at a low point.

Confederate soldiers were treated to the best accommodations on their return to New Orleans, many of them housed at the St. Charles. What these returning soldiers didn't have too much of, though, was ready money, and the hotel racked up $30,000 worth of bills that were never settled. A short boom period followed until around 1868, which buoyed the hotel slightly, but hard times lay ahead. In 1878, the hotel underwent extensive repairs, expanding its capacity to somewhere between six and seven hundred guests over four hundred bedrooms.

The fate of the second St. Charles Hotel was well signposted. As John Kendall tells it in his 1922 *History of New Orleans*:

PICTURE GALLERY

MAIN RESTAURANT

MUSIC ROOM

EMPIRE PARLOR

MEN'S CAFE

BILLIARD ROOM

A booklet with interior views of the rooms of the St. Charles Hotel, 1917. *Printed in "Souvenir of New Orleans: The City Care Forgot," 3rd edition, published by the St. Charles Hotel, New Orleans, 1917.*

NEW ORLEANS HISTORIC HOTELS

> *A serious fire in 1876 did extensive damage to the hotel; another on October 3, 1880, when damage estimated at $25,000 was done; and finally, on April 28, 1894, the building was entirely consumed. It is rather a remarkable fact that only in the last fire was there any known loss of life. In 1851, several people were slightly injured. In the last fire, however, four persons perished, and a number were more or less slightly injured. The present building was erected immediately after the fire.*

The "present building" to which Kendall refers was up and running in 1895 and was built without replication of the Greek Revival style, the architects instead opting for a Beaux Arts look. The hotel business was starting to see increased levels of competition in New Orleans as the twentieth century came around, and the St. Charles consolidated its luxury amenities, a step that didn't go unnoticed in the 1902 guide to New Orleans published by the Honorable James S. Zacharie:

> *When the present twelve-story and basement addition is complete, the St. Charles will be one of the very largest and one of the finest houses in the country, with accommodations for more than a thousand guests, and with upwards of four hundred rooms having private bath connections. It is fireproof, steam-heated and lighted throughout with electricity. The drinking water is filtered, distilled and aerated, and the ice made from it on the premises.*
>
> *The Palm Garden is the largest, and one of the finest in the country, and is specially suited for Dances, Weddings, Receptions, Banquets, Dinner and Supper Parties. The Colonnade and Palm Garden afford a delightful resting place and promenade, in sunshine and shade. The Turkish and Russian Baths are of marble, with every modern convenience for comfort and luxury, and with experienced massage operators, chiropodists and manicureists in attendance. The Hotel is modern, first-class and kept up to the highest standard in all departments.*

The hotel was also stepping up its publicity operations. The following advertisement appeared in *The* Picayune's Guide to *New Orleans* in 1904 and laid out the luxuries afforded to the hotel's guests:

> *Visit Quaint, Historic New Orleans and the New St. Charles Hotel. It is one of the latest, largest and best hotels in the country. It is the only fireproof hotel in the city. It is steam-heated and lighted throughout with electricity.*

NEW ORLEANS HISTORIC HOTELS

A postcard of a view of the St. Charles Hotel at the corner of Gravier Street and St. Charles Avenue, 1919. *No publisher listed*.

> *The drinking water is filtered, distilled and aerated; it and the ice made from it on the premises are absolutely pure. The Colonnade and Covered Roof Garden offer a delightful promenade. The Turkish and Russian baths are among the finest in the country, built of marble and luxuriously fitted up, with experienced massage operators in attendance. The hotel is kept on both the American and European plans.*

In 1912, the hotel embarked on a national marketing campaign that actually coined a nickname for New Orleans. It was at this time that the St. Charles began to bill New Orleans as "The City That Care Forgot," a nicely ambiguous turn of phrase that soon became subsumed in the national lexicon.

Back home, the *Daily Picayune* ran a four-column advert that read: "New Orleans. The City that care forgot. The St Charles. The center of the city's hotel life." This campaign soon went national, with newspapers from Des Moines and Philadelphia adding: "The St. Charles. Finest all year hotel in the south." The advert was backed up with a well-produced souvenir photo booklet, *The City That Care Forgot*, which by 1917 had reached its third edition.

The hotel maintained its prestige for much of the first half of the twentieth century, still managing to attract celebrities, politicians, royalty and heads of state. A slow deterioration from around 1950 was noticeable, though, as the ever-increasing competition from large modern hotels took its toll.

Even a takeover by the Sheraton Hotel Group in 1959 did little to halt the decline. At this time, the hotel had a tiki bar called the Outrigger, with "authentic" Polynesian décor and exotic drinks, which operated alongside the longstanding Café de Paris. These outlets did little to improve custom, and Sheraton sold the property in 1965.

The third incarnation of this grand old hotel, which had survived and come back from so much for so long, finally gave up the ghost in 1974, closing its doors and facing demolition for the final time.

Lagniappe

Presidents McKinley, Roosevelt and Taft were among the hotel's guests.

Among his observations, Lafcadio Hearn also mentions the Gold Service of the hotel—a dinner service of such quality that it was said to be worth over $16,000 and only ever used on extremely special occasions. It's little wonder that Hearn more than once referred to the Crescent City as El Dorado.

One of the occasions on which the gold service was used was at the "stag" of October 30, 1882, in honor of the Irish statesman Alexander Sullivan. There were eight courses, including dozens of dishes and the finest of wines. Ten formal toasts were made, with guests sitting down to dinner at 8:00 p.m. and not finishing until 1:00 a.m.

When it opened in 1837, the St. Charles was the first hotel in New Orleans to admit unaccompanied women. Before this time, ladies had to seek refuge in the city's boardinghouses.

The ladies' parlor in the second St. Charles Hotel was a truly magnificent affair. The furniture bill ran to $15,000, and it housed the largest mirrors ever to be imported into the United States.

As the hotel passed into the twentieth century, modernity took ahold at times, much to the horror of some observers. A *Times-Picayune* editorial decries the removal in 1957 of the brass plates that denoted the "Ladies' Entrance," and a particularly acerbic 1959 column in the *New Orleans States and Item* warns the Sheraton company (which had acquired the property by this time) against "amputating the venerable and historic name of the St. Charles Hotel by calling it the Sheraton-Charles."

3.
THE NEW ASTOR HOTEL (FORMERLY THE COSMOPOLITAN HOTEL)

The place was noted for its bar as well as its cuisine and over meals washed down by suitable liquids, many a Central American revolution was hatched by Spanish speaking guests.
—Stanley Arthur, A History of the Vieux Carré

As you'll soon come to realize, almost everyone involved in commerce and hotel life in the early days of the French Quarter was called Jean-Baptiste. The original owner of what was then 13–15 Royal Street (and then 121–123 Royal Street) was no exception, being a businessman by the name of Jean-Baptiste Solari.

The name may be familiar to older New Orleans residents as Solari's family went on to found and run the famous food store that bore the family name, also with a branch right on Royal Street that boasted, among other things, a "cheese cave" and a 1,600-bottle wine cellar.

Solari was obviously a man of vision—his descendants would one day invent cheese caves, after all—and in 1891, he commissioned Thomas Sully to build him a five-and-a-half-story building. The *Daily States* report from September 22, 1891, reads: "On Royal between Canal and Customhouse, there is in the process of construction a magnificent five storied building which is destined for hotel purposes."

The unnamed journalist expresses an understandable fear that as the bay windows are made of wood, a fire could easily break out, fires being seemingly a daily occurrence in the Quarter at this time. However, city engineer B.M. Howard reassured the newspaper, saying the intention was to "cover them with galvanized sheet iron."

With the public's fears assuaged, in 1892, Solari opened said building as the Cosmopolitan Hotel and Café Restaurant, because it presumably paid to hedge your bets when naming a business. The *Daily Picayune* from January 1892 remarks on the "handsome new five-storey [*sic*] building on the site of a famous old hostelry [presumably the Cosmopolitan Restaurant], in the hotel [being] 24 rooms, etc…"

Not only was the hotel extremely aesthetically pleasing, with its iron columns, vestibule covered in Belgian mosaics and windows of multicolored glass, but it also had function underlying its graceful form. It was one of the first hotels in the city, for example, to offer guests electric lights and filtered water, immediately setting itself up as a luxury boutique hotel before the term even existed. At this time, a newspaper advertisement just read: "Near Canal Street. Elevator. European plan, $1.50 and up."

The stained-glass windows, by the way, paid homage to three of the city's famed residents. In *Old New Orleans*, Stanley Arthur describes them thus:

> *Two were native sons, Paul Morphy and Ferdinand Gottschalk. For Morphy, peer of chess players, one window shows chessmen on a checkerboard. A second window depicting "The Last Hope" on a sheet of music is a tribute to Gottschalk, famed organist and composer. The third window picturing a singing mocking bird honors John James Audubon who, though not born in La., made in this state most of the bird drawings that bought him imperishable fame.*

Chandeliers, ceiling fans and some of the finest food in the Quarter cemented its reputation, and as the world ushered in the twentieth century, the Cosmopolitan was enjoying a glorious heyday. It was especially popular with the political classes but had such a wide-ranging appeal that it had already opened an extension, doubling its size by adding an annex behind the original building facing onto Bourbon Street.

The two entrances provided cover for hotel clientele who may not have been as welcome among the well-to-do guests. In her 2001 book, *The Last Madam: A Life in the New Orleans Underground*, Christine Wiltz relates tales of Norma Wallis, one of the city's most renowned streetwalkers.

Wiltz had this to say about the hotel:

> *The Cosmopolitan Hotel, a half block off Canal Street, had addresses on both Bourbon and Royal Streets—its lobby ran straight through the entire*

> *block. The Cosmopolitan catered to the affluent. It had a reputation as a family hotel. The ladies' entrance was on Royal Street, but, as Norma observed, not all the women who used it were ladies—except of the night.*

In *A History of the Vieux Carré*, Stanley Arthur notes, somewhat intriguingly: "The building…[was] a favorite rendezvous in the gay '90s for gourmets and society folk. The place was noted for its bar as well as its cuisine and over meals washed down by suitable liquids, many a Central American revolution was hatched by Spanish speaking guests."

In 1925, having been renamed the New Astor, the hotel was still garnering press. The *New Orleans Item* of December 25, 1925, makes some complimentary, if joyless, notes: "The building is tall and very shallow, with rooms commodious and with very high ceilings with arches over the center, surrounding a curved stairway over which, at the top of the five stories, a skylight shines and each room has a private bath and is steam heated. All rooms have bay windows."

The report goes on to mention the history of the building, though, and it transpires that guests are staying on very hallowed ground, depending on how they felt about Napoleon. Some further facts came from the *New Orleans Item*:

> *The New Astor Hotel is run by O.W. Zeagler. Before The Astor came into being, the building was The Cosmopolitan Hotel and was for some 50 years the making and breaking of Louisiana politicians. Before that time it was the residence of Dr. Antommarchi, physician to Napoleon Bonaparte, who came to New Orleans after the tragedy of Waterloo, and who practiced here for many years.*

There are several points to address here. Firstly, even though I am an Englishman, as a gentleman, I will let slide the description of the outcome of the Battle of Waterloo as "the tragedy." Secondly, it's interesting that the place was known as a pressure cooker for the politicos of the day and gives the place more than a whiff of scandal. The last point—that the hotel stands on what was previously the residence of Dr. François Antommarchi—is an obvious one to expand on.

In 1819, a high-society merchant, David Urquhart, bought the building from one William Kenner for $13,000. He upgraded the property significantly, replenishing the interiors with fine materials and adding amenities such as a kitchen, stable and outhouses.

NEW ORLEANS HISTORIC HOTELS

When Dr. Antommarchi arrived in New Orleans in 1834, he was received with some celebration, having been closely associated with the (in the locals' eyes) heroic Bonaparte. He was serenaded, toasted and, although he was, as we have heard, housed at L'Hôtel des Etrangers for a short time, he soon moved into this prestigious residence on Royal Street.

Antommarchi brought with him, it eventually transpired, a great treasure in the form of one of only four casts of Napoleon's death mask, having attended to the exiled warrior on Saint Helena and recording his death in 1821.

He donated the mask to the city, endearing him to the place even more. The transfer (which took place on November 23, 1834) was an elaborate affair, with a procession of city elders and statesmen marching to the house accompanied by a legion of soldiers, who gave a 101-gun salute as the mask was handed over. Anyone can see the mask to this day without any pomp or ceremony, as it is on display in the Cabildo museum.

The doctor was so well loved in New Orleans that he decided to stay on, eventually setting up a medical practice in the building next door to the Urquhart residence. He lived and worked in the city until 1838, when he moved to Mexico and then shortly after to Cuba, where he died.

Sadly, the hotel's days of success and political trial by fire seemed to come to an end while the twentieth century had barely gotten underway. The reasons aren't well documented, though we can suppose the growing number of alternatives in the CBD and the run-down nature of the French Quarter at that time had something to contribute to the state of affairs.

The Bourbon Street annex was demolished in the 1940s, and the Royal Street building, although still upright to this day, has been derelict since the early 1970s. Plans to construct a new Cosmopolitan Hotel have regularly been touted, but at the time of writing, nothing has yet transpired.

LAGNIAPPE

Antoine Amédée Peychaud, the famous dispenser of the distinctive bitters, ran his apothecary/pharmacy at 437 Royal Street (the current address), which was, *before* the renumbering of the streets, 123 Royal Street.

4.
MAISON DE VILLE

Most of the confidence which I appear to feel, especially when influenced by noon wine, is only a pretense.
—*Tennessee Williams*

In his book *Old New Orleans: A History of the Vieux Carré, Its Ancient and Historical Buildings*, Stanley Arthur puts the construction of the building at 727 Toulouse Street at around 1800. Actually, Mr. Arthur says this is when the building was "erected," meaning that construction could feasibly have been going on for some time, putting the date somewhere between Mr. Arthur's and the date that the hotel suggests for the building, 1793.

This latter date is when the first records of local builder Jean Baptiste Lille Sarpy start to show up, although independent surveys on some of the techniques used in the mortar of the former slave quarters put the original buildings (of which very few examples remain thanks to the relentless successions of fires in the Quarter) as perhaps some fifty years older. This, then, would make them among the oldest standing structures in the city and possibly the state.

Whichever way you look at it, the building is an old one, even for the French Quarter. These oldest buildings are probably examples of what were known as *garçonnières*, which were the quarters where Creole families would have their grown, unmarried sons live until they found wives and moved on—kind of an early version of living in your parents' basement.

An inventory of the building from 1800 describes it in tediously factual detail as "a house of brick and wood, which is inhabited by the defunct and his family, terrace roofed, at the corner of Toulouse and Bourbon, built on a lot 70' in front and 80' of depth, to which has been added the two lots that goes with the house in Toulouse Street."

Not too much is documented about the Lille Sarpy family, short of that they constructed a one-story building on the land and, charmingly, that they were heavily involved in the slave trade. Jean Baptiste died in 1798, leaving the house to his son, Jean Baptiste Jr., who died suddenly not too long after that.

The son's wife, Marie-Josèphe "Pouponne" Díaz (the nickname is Haitian and means, roughly, "the one who looks after babies") promptly suffered a nervous breakdown, and it was at this time that Sarpy Jr.'s daughter, Henriette de Lille, inherited the family home.

Henriette was of a very strong religious persuasion, and after making sure that her mother was provided for, she sold off the entirety of the family's assets and founded her own order of nuns, named the Sisters of the Presentation. The order was composed of free women of color and provided nursing care for orphans and, later, schooling.

A side note: Although unrecognized at the time, the order was vindicated in 1989 when the Vatican canonized Henriette de Lille. She was declared venerable (officially "heroic in virtue" which is one level below sainthood) in 2010. This has little bearing on the hotel's history, but it's an interesting diversion nonetheless, and if you wander around the Tremé neighborhood, you'll see she has a street named for her.

The early nineteenth century was when the French Quarter as we know it was really beginning to find its shape and style, and in this neighborhood, that was in no little measure thanks to the architects Joseph Guillot and Claude Gurlie.

These fine men owned and developed swathes of property along Toulouse, Royal and Decatur Streets, and in their whirlwind of transformation, they turned what had been a single-story family home at 727 Toulouse into a three-story mansion, with balconies and the signature wood cornice that adorns the roof of the Maison de Ville.

Meanwhile, over in France, Napoleon had been keeping himself busy being exiled to Saint Helena, and many of his supporters and military leaders fled the country, a sizeable number of them to New Orleans. One such immigrant was the former head of Napoleon's cavalry corps, Jean-Baptiste Benjamin Vignié.

There's a very euphemistic act of sale dated 1812 that puts Vignié as the owner of a "privateer" ship named *Pandoure* and further goes on to list a discussion about the "division of the spoils," so it's a forgivable leap to make

NEW ORLEANS HISTORIC HOTELS

Each delightful bedroom opens onto a gallery or patio

A corner of the Lobby looking into the Card Room

Hotel Maison de Ville offers New Orleans' most distinctive hospitality

Hotel Maison de Ville in the heart of the Vieux Carre is as luxurious and exclusive as a private club. It is ideally located in the midst of famous restaurants and fascinating antique shops. Its beautifully furnished bedrooms, with private baths, will give you the utmost in comfort. You will enjoy its charming patio and old world atmosphere.

FOR RESERVATIONS
WRITE MRS. MADELINE J. EHRLICH, PROPRIETOR • 727 TOULOUSE STREET, NEW ORLEANS, LOUISIANA
PHONE: MA 1189

From a brochure for the Maison de Ville, 1950s.

if we assume that at least some casual piracy was a component of this man's post-Napoloeonic life. The 727 Toulouse address was and is a very handy location for Pirate's Alley, which is just three blocks away, after all.

In any case, Mr. Vignié is listed as the building's owner in 1826, Guillot and Gurlie having spliced up the block between them to sell off to interested parties. Vignié sold the place some three years later, and the house bounced around a succession of owners, none of whom seem to have connections to piracy or, indeed, any interesting stories whatsoever.

That cannot be said, however, of some of the building's residents. One early such person was a chemist (in those days known as apothecary) by the name of Antoine Amédé Peychaud. Although most apothecaries worked out of laboratories in their places of residence, Peychaud had a separate workspace, around the corner on Royal Street.

Peychaud did not revolutionize the medical profession, though he did bring something revolutionary into the world—that is, the world of cocktails. Up until the 1830s, cocktails as we know them didn't really exist beyond the odd primitive punch or cobbler.

Peychaud had developed a line of alcoholic herbal bitters, which he had been unsurprisingly prescribing to people as a tonic for all manner of ailments. He sometimes presented his bitters mixed into a serving of brandy or cognac in an eggcup, or *coquetier*.

As the drink gained popularity, it evolved into what the cocktail world now knows as the Sazerac, taking its name from one of the original recipes that used the cognac Sazerac de Forge et Fils. It is now a whiskey cocktail, served in bars all over New Orleans, though if you'd care to make your own, there's a recipe included in the appendices.

To quote the official Sazerac Company from its website: "By 1850, the Sazerac Cocktail, made with Sazerac French brandy and Peychaud's Bitters, was immensely popular, and became the first 'branded' cocktail. In 1873, the recipe for the Sazerac Cocktail was altered to replace the French brandy with American Rye whiskey, and a dash of absinthe was added."

In the meantime, the house had been bought by Mrs. Marie Anne Lucas Blondeau and then, on her death in 1857, passed to her offspring, Adélard and Henriette Blondeau. Henriette was a real woman about town, known as the "Dusky Socialite" and known as an expert hairdresser.

Blondeau is remembered in the memoir *Social Life in Old New Orleans, Being Recollections of My Girlhood* by Eliza Ripley. "Dusky Blondeau comes," remembers Miss Ripley with seemingly no little excitement, "with her *tignon* [headdress] stuck full of pins and the deep pockets of her apron bulging with sticks of bandoline pots of pomade, hairpins and a comb to dress the hair of the mademoiselle."

Miss Ripley isn't done yet, as she runs into her dusky beautician some years later. "We all remember Henriette Blondeau," she recalls. "She dressed my sisters hair in the early [eighteen] forties and she dressed mine ten years later, and I met her in the hall of the St. Charles Hotel, plying her trade, the same Henriette, with the same ample apron, the tools of her trade sticking out from her pockets."

NEW ORLEANS HISTORIC HOTELS

Lounge at the Maison de Ville. *Paul Oswell.*

This profession was an honorable one for free women of color. The famous voodoo priestess Marie Leveau, for instance, spent her days practicing just such an innocent line of work, styling the hair of her many white clients.

The house was with the Blondeau family until 1871, when it again began a life of relatively anonymous ownership, for many years the property of various families, banks and realty developers.

It isn't until 1944 that the story of the modern-day hotel really begins. The owners at this time are Alexander Wylie and Mary A. McDougal. Mary had made the acquaintance of a travel agent by the name of Madeline Erlich, who was visiting New Orleans for the first time.

As Mary showed her new friend around her home, Ms. Erlich was immediately bowled over by the beauty of the courtyard and fell in love even more as she heard the stories of Peychaud. At that time, there were no hotels that really captured the romance of the old French Quarter, and Ms. Erlich implored Mary and her husband to move into a smaller house and turn the property at 727 Toulouse into a hotel.

After some persuasion, the couple agreed, and moved out, turning their former home into a small hotel and installing Ms. Erlich as manager of the business. That situation worked out pretty well for her, all in all. I'm sure her motives were pure. She did in fact throw herself into finding the best fixtures and fitting for the new hotel, her finest find being a door from the old St. Louis (now Omni Royal Orleans) Hotel, salvaged from the 1915 hurricane. The door graces the doorway to the hotel to this very day.

The hotel was fondly thought of and gained a loyal customer base—the current owner reports that as the hotel was rebuilt and restored during its current incarnation, people would stop by and regale them with tales of how they spent their honeymoon there or celebrated an anniversary.

Many hotels in New Orleans claim the patronage of local literary heroes, but Maison de Ville has televisual proof of one of its most famous residents. The playwright Tennessee Williams eventually bought his own home in New Orleans on Dumaine Street, but previous to this, he would often stay in Room 9 of the Mason de Ville (now the Tennessee Williams suite).

The owner likes to suggest that Williams often sat in the courtyard drinking Sazeracs, hardly an unreasonable assumption, and it's a reassuring image that encapsulates the history of the building—paying homage to Mr. Peychaud—very nicely. If he could also be reported to be tending

This photo is of Tennessee Williams (left) and Dick Cavett (right) recording the *Dick Cavett Show* in the courtyard of the Maison de Ville Hotel in 1974.

to someone's hair or dividing up the spoils from a recent piracy, then the romance would be complete.

It is also claimed that Williams completed his most famous work, *A Streetcar Named Desire*, while staying in the cottage, a claim backed up by the Tennessee Williams Society, which also says that Room 9 was his abode of choice. On its website, the society notes, "When Williams wasn't renting, he would frequent his favorite hotels. Room #9 was his room of choice at the Hotel Maison de Ville, located at 727 Toulouse St. In was in that lovely interior courtyard that Williams found a peaceful setting to pen the drama of *Streetcar Name Desire* and other works."

What is undeniable is that the courtyard bore witness to one of Williams's television appearances. In August 1974, the writer was interviewed there by Dick Cavett, recording a ninety-minute show for ABC Television.

The hotel enjoyed popularity for many years before eventually falling, if not into actual disrepair, then at least a period of stagnation. In 2012, after a period of renovation and repair, the hotel was reopened. It now enjoys a new, improved standard of accommodation and luxury, with impressively appointed period rooms and cottages around the courtyard—where Antoine Peychaud and Tennessee Williams once enjoyed their evening libations—sensitively modernized and once again welcoming discerning guests.

Lagniappe

As well as Peychaud and Williams, there have been a wealth of famous and celebrity guests that have stayed at the Maison de Ville. Elizabeth Taylor, Robert Redford, Lady Bird Johnson, Dan Akroyd, Paul McCartney, Michael Jackson and Spike Lee are included on the roll of honor.

Cottage four is said to be haunted by a military man with a penchant for a particular kind of music. A hotel employee is said to have opened the door to show a guest into the room only to find a man dressed in a 1940s military uniform who promptly disappeared. Reports say that when the cottage's radio is tuned to any station, the ghost changes it back to a country station, which is strange as you'd think New Orleans ghosts would prefer jazz. In any case, there are stories of him materializing fully "when séances are held" and also appearing as a solid, live person before walking through walls. His voice has been recorded by investigators saying, "I need to leave," which is especially true since there's no record of his arranging a late check out. Film and video crews have allegedly captured a glimpse of him or flashes of his uniform and medals.

Various ghost tours also say that guests have reported seeing mysterious wet footprints and women and men dressed in vintage clothing. There's also the usual litany of paranormal goings on: nightly rapping noises, moving objects, disembodied voices and, more inconveniently, sheets pulled off in the middle of the night.

The hotel has more than one connection to cocktails and the spirits industry. The current owner, Mr. Richard Poe II, also owns the Dos Lunas Tequila company.

The Sazerac has come a long way since the days of Peychaud and is now, in fact, the official state cocktail of Louisiana. At the time of this writing, no other states even had an official state cocktail. As a point of reference, and marking an important cultural difference, the official state beverage of Ohio, for example, is tomato juice.

5.
THE ROOSEVELT
(FORMERLY THE GRUNEWALD AND THE FAIRMONT)

Senator Huey P. Long went to New York, bringing along the Roosevelt's head bartender. Long attacked President Roosevelt's New Deal while simultaneously instructing the crowd on the finer points of the gin fizz.
—Sally Asher

As the Civil War came to an end, many talented people who had left New Orleans or been displaced began to return to the city. One of these was German architect Charles Lewis Hillger, who found himself immediately in demand, designing and building (with his former apprentice Frederick Reusch) private houses and churches as the city began the lengthy process of reconstruction.

Fellow Bavarian and entrepreneur Louis Grunewald commissioned Hillger to build a performing arts center, and this he did in some style. Grunewald Hall sat just off Canal Street on Baronne Street and was a palatial entertainment center, designed and built in a Bavarian Baroque style. As well as a beautiful concert hall, the building contained music stores and showrooms selling everything from sheet music to instruments, and its grand front entrance graced Canal Street with some panache.

The venue was a huge success, riding the rapid wave of gentrification in the area and playing host to some of the city's biggest classical music performances of the day. It was a great cultural center and meeting place for the city's large German population, whose members were enthusiastically involved in the music scene of the day.

NEW ORLEANS HISTORIC HOTELS

The modern-day Roosevelt Hotel exterior.

Sadly, the music hall was destroyed by fire in 1892, and Louis Grunewald decided to reopen as a hotel. And so it was that in 1893, the Grunewald Hotel opened in the Baronne Street location. This first incarnation was, with typical Grunewaldian flair, a lavish building some six stories high and with two hundred or so rooms.

The hotel was an immediate success, so much so that Grunewald, ever the ambitious businessman, decided on a daring large-scale expansion. By 1900, he was looking into the acquisition of the building's adjoining properties, and over time, he successfully negotiated their purchase. On New Year's Eve 1907, a brand-new, four-hundred-room, fourteen-story annex opened, expanding the Grunewald to three times its former size and in the process, planting a huge German flag on the high-end hotel scene in New Orleans.

One very significant feature of this new hotel was the Cave. Essentially the hotel's bar, it is arguably the first nightclub to operate in the United States and is even more remarkable given its extravagant interior design. Grunewald had created a magical, grotto-like place, with elaborate plaster rock formations, painted nymphs and models of gnomes. It was a popular drinking spot from the day it opened.

This being New Orleans, drinking was a huge part of the city's social life, as it is now, and so the shadow of Prohibition loomed larger for people here than perhaps it did elsewhere in the country.

The hotel tried to adapt as business became more difficult. The Cave would play host to glamorous midnight shows, jazz bands and chorus girls entertaining the hotel guests until the early hours. The public bars were converted to serve soft drinks, and business was as normal as it could be under the circumstances.

In her essay *Weathering a Dry Spell*, writer Sally Asher describes one dramatic event at the hotel during those Prohibition years:

> *During the Grain Dealers' Association Conference at the hotel* [in 1922], *Prohibition agents busted in on rooms 1263 and 1265 to find full bars with no less than 27 barrels of beer and many bottles of Sazerac cocktails and Scotch. It took four trucks to haul away the contraband. The following day, someone hung a wreath on room 1265 with a placard: "DIED. The whole Damn Barley Corn Family. The remains may be viewed at the home of their tender Uncle Sam. Mourners. Hangovers. Expectant Heirs are invited to attend services." One guest stated that the rooms would forever be a sacred sanctuary.*

There is no direct link to this and the closure of the hotel the following year, but the ban on alcohol couldn't have helped business. Nevertheless, the hotel was sold and extensively remodeled, and in 1923, a new hotel was constructed and named the Roosevelt in honor of the late former president Theodore Roosevelt. This new, even more opulent incarnation now boasted 505 rooms and spanned an entire city block.

The new business needed the good times to roll, one way or another. To continue social life as best it could, the hotel offered dances in its new ballrooms, the Venetian Room and the Fountain Room. It served up 'Sazerac cocktails', which were, disappointingly, just glasses of ginger ale.

The Sazerac Bar at the Roosevelt Hotel.

This was a wise choice, given some of the hotel's regular guests, as Sally Asher goes on to note:

> *Prohibition Agent No. 1 Isadore "Izzy" Einstein and his partner Peter Reager liked to stay at the Roosevelt while in New Orleans. Newspapers announced their arrival practically as tips for bootleggers to avoid being busted. The men registered under assumed names and disguised themselves as prize fighters, laborers and fruit peddlers, and they even brought women along to further their ruse. The men also brought results: in ten days during the winter of 1923, they led more than 45 raids. The Roosevelt wasn't among them.*

Thankfully, this all came to an end on December 5, 1933. That very evening, the food and beverage purchasing manager accepted the city's first legal delivery of whiskey, and the cameras flashed as he opened it and ushered back in the celebratory times that the hotel had known in its Grunewald days.

More alcoholic developments were quick to follow. Just before Prohibition had come on, the city had become enamored of a creation of a local bartender, Henry Ramos. His cocktail—the Ramos Gin Fizz—had become a hit, and lines of people would form to buy a glass of this wonderful new drink. (Reports from 1915 have people waiting an hour in line as dozens of "shaker boys" tried to prepare the drinks as fast as they could to keep up with demand).

Ramos had quit the bar business and published his recipe in a fit of pique as Prohibition took hold so that his creation might live on. In 1934, the Roosevelt announced that it had acquired exclusive rights to the drink, and would be the only place in New Orleans dispensing it. This was quite a coup, given its popularity.

Never one to miss out on a photo or publicity opportunity, the controversial senator Huey P. Long took advantage of his growing ties to the hotel. Sally Asher describes the developments and Long's natural sense of outrageous showmanship: "[In 1935] Senator Huey P. Long went to New York, bringing along the Roosevelt's head bartender. Long attacked President Roosevelt's New Deal while simultaneously instructing the crowd on the finer points of the gin fizz, thus further ushering the hotel into legend."

By 1934, one of Long's close confidants and advisers had taken control of the Roosevelt. The rise of Seymour Weiss is a tale of a true American dream. Weiss had started out as the lowly manager of the hotel barbershop when the property had opened in 1923. With just a year passed, he had already been promoted to assistant manager of the hotel, eventually becoming manager in 1928.

As if this ascent to power wasn't heady enough, in 1931, Weiss was named president of the New Orleans Roosevelt Group, meaning that he was now the principal owner and managing director of the hotel, a quite unbelievable career trajectory in anyone's book. His leadership wasn't a flash in the pan, either—he held the position until 1965.

Weiss was a longtime supporter of Long, and it was no surprise that he allowed the governor and then senator to set up his headquarters in the Roosevelt Hotel. It was said that one of Weiss's main jobs was just keeping Long from getting lost in the maze of hotel corridors, and he must have done this effectively as he was considered one of Long's right-hand men. Weiss was one of the few people present at Long's deathbed as he passed away following a successful assassination attempt in 1935.

Weiss was an incredibly successful hotelier. According to his Wikipedia page, he was an active member of the American Hotel Association and

The Storming of the Sazerac Bar in 1949.

was president of both the Louisiana Hotel-Motel and the New Orleans Hotel associations, winning statewide awards for hotel management in 1952 and 1957.

It was during Weiss's time that two of the hotel's most famous venues made their mark. The Blue Room opened in 1935, and the Sazerac Bar opened in 1949, both playing host to all manner of high-society parties and iconic moments, the latter famously undergoing the "Storming of the Sazerac Bar."

To celebrate the Sazerac Bar moving to the Roosevelt Hotel (it had previously been located on Carondalet and Gravier Streets), the hotel allowed women to drink whenever they liked for the first time. Up until this point, they had only been allowed in the bar once a year—on Mardi Gras. The day produced one of the era's classic photos, with well-dressed women crowding the place, lining up to order one of the signature cocktails.

The Blue Room, with its brocade walls, columns and chandeliers, was equally renowned and welcomed some of the most famous performers of the twentieth century, including Ella Fitzgerald, Judy Garland, Tina

Turner, Jimmy Durante and Carol Channing and more. At one time it even featured a temporary ice-skating rink. The best-loved performers, though, were always the big bands, among them the Leon Kelner Orchestra, which became a local institution, and the Glen Miller Band, which enjoyed a ten-week engagement in the Blue Room in the 1930s.

Under Weiss's expert guidance, the hotel flourished during this time and was a leading player in New Orleans's social scene. In 1965, the hotel was sold to the Fairmont Group, which made the peculiar decision—given the hotel's long-standing success and the affection in which it was held locally and nationally—to rename it the Fairmont.

It may seem a strange choice to rename the hotel and not trade on the good name and prestige of the Roosevelt, but at this time in New Orleans, there was a near-rabid fashion to have everything new, to dissociate from the past and reinvent the city. This seems a foreign concept in today's city, where every effort is made, through naming and marketing, to make the oldest possible connections.

Thus began a relatively uneventful but steady fifty years. Following the 2005 levee failures during Hurricane Katrina, the hotel sustained enough damage to close it down, and it would remain closed for four years. The hotel was sold again, this time to the Waldorf Astoria Group, which looked to restore it to its former glory. The renovation of the newly renamed

A postcard for the Blue Room at Roosevelt Hotel.

Roosevelt New Orleans ultimately cost over $150 million, the largest private post-Katrina investment in downtown New Orleans.

The Roosevelt proudly reopened its doors on July 1, 2009. The Sazerac Bar, Blue Room and many of the original fixtures and fittings were once again ready to welcome guests, and the hotel has quickly restored not only some of the original ambience but also its reputation as a classic New Orleans hotel in the minds of locals and loyal guests alike.

Lagniappe

In the lobby is a rosewood grand piano, built in the nineteenth century by Gaveau Pianos, one of the largest manufacturers in France at that time. This remarkable instrument was sold in the early 1900s by Basile Barès, who was born into servitude in 1845 to Adolph Périer of New Orleans and grew up working in Périer's French Quarter piano shop, where Barès learned to play. In 1866, six years after composing his own music and despite laws limiting slaves' rights at the time, Barès was granted a musical copyright, becoming the first slave ever to receive such a license.

The hotel has hosted legendary characters famous and infamous, including Marlene Dietrich, Audrey Hepburn, Grace Kelly, Louis Armstrong, Cab Calloway, Ray Charles, Jack Benny and Bob Hope. Louisiana governor Huey P. Long used his twelfth-floor suite at the hotel as his base of operations when he was in the city.

The Sazerac Bar was built and decorated with Art Deco motifs, the bar's standout features being four remarkable murals created during the 1930s by Paul Ninas. Though extremely diverse, the artistic style of that time, referred to as "social realism," frequently focused on the period's economic hardships and working-class people performing their jobs.

Near the entrance stands the hotel's signature clock, one of the largest known conical pendulum timepieces and made for the Paris Exhibitions of 1867 and 1878. Today, it proudly welcomes guests and the community and provides an opportunity for dignitaries to wind its delicate timekeeping mechanism.

A box containing over $1 million could be hidden somewhere in the property. As Huey Long lay on his deathbed, Seymour Weiss asked him where something called the "Dedcut Box" was, a receptacle containing a vast amount of campaign funds, collected in cash. "I'll tell you later, Seymour" said Long before promptly dying. The box has never been found.

Teddy Bear Tea, another holiday tradition begun in the 1990s, is held in an exquisite ballroom decorated with Santa's workshop. Meeting Santa, receiving their very own teddy bear, taking part in caroling and fairy tale storytelling—these are just a few of the activities that allow families to welcome and celebrate the holidays.

For the first time in a half century, the "R" that formed the centerpiece of the Roosevelt's elaborate coat of arms for most of its life is visible again throughout the hotel while the bust of President Teddy Roosevelt, for whom the hotel is named, beams a warm welcome at the Baronne Street entrance.

Elvis Presley was a guest at the hotel while he filmed *King Creole* in 1958, using a back stairway to escape the enormous crowds that greeted him outside the hotel.

Among the many films shot at the Roosevelt are *Ray*, which depicted the life of singer Ray Charles; *All the King's Men*, loosely based on the hotel's favorite son, Governor Huey P. Long; *The Twilight Saga: Breaking Dawn*; and the TNT television series *Memphis Beat*.

For a time in 1938, the Blue Room became the Hawaiian Blue Room and resembled a tropical oasis, replete with palm trees, moving clouds, stars in the ceiling and even a rain simulator.

6.
AUDUBON COTTAGES

Hopes are but shy birds flying at a great distance, seldom reached by the best of guns.
—*John James Audubon*

You don't need to be a historian, ornithologist or hotel naming consultant to guess who stayed here at some point. John James Audubon, graduating from the boarding room next door, apparently stayed here with his family in the early 1820s, saying about the move, "The dingy old structure with its low sloping roof and green shutters is in a bad state of repair, but despite its age it appears to be still a sturdy building."

Thankfully, he had his bird hunting and art to distract him, though it is said that at this time, he was facing near starvation and was "feverishly" working on his paintings. Let's hope that the Audubon family had moved a suitably sensible distance away by the 1880s, as the address was then achieving a reputation that would not go down in history as anything approaching high art.

In his 1936 book, *The French Quarter: An Informal History of the New Orleans Underworld*, author Herbert Asbury relates the following charming information about the address (then 111 Dauphine as it was before the renumbering of the French Quarter):

> At No. 111 Dauphine Street was a brothel, which was described by the Picayune *in 1885 as the worst Negro dive in the city, and which at that time was the particular haunt of Red Light Liz, the sweetheart of Joe the Whipper and a noted brawler. In earlier days, however, the house had been occupied by white prostitutes, and gained considerable renown by reason of*

NEW ORLEANS HISTORIC HOTELS

A view of the courtyard of the Audubon Cottages.

> *the tragic end of one of its inmates, Nellie Gaspar; and the mere presence of another, a woman known as "the notorious Fanny Peel."*

Red Light Liz and Joe the Whipper do sound like a match made in heaven, you have to admit. It's almost a shame that Audubon wasn't obsessed with painting all the prostitutes in New Orleans—he could have done it without leaving his doorstep and with far less purchasing of bullets.

Fanny Peel was, according to Asbury's information, "the most beautiful courtesan who ever appeared in New Orleans." She was the daughter of a preacher and the graduate of a female seminary, which were obviously the perfect foundations for a career in prostitution at the age of fifteen. By the time she arrived in New Orleans, she had already seen the high life in New York and Chicago, so it didn't go especially well for her, as Mr. Asbury notes:

> *She came to New Orleans in 1857 with her coachman, a free Negro, whom she immediately sold as a slave to a Louisiana planter. She entered the brothel at No. 111 Dauphine Street, but was soon dismissed because she refused to have anything to do with the men who visited the place—she said they weren't good enough for her. She went to Mobile early in 1858 and died there during the summer of that year.*

Interior of one of the cottages at Audubon Cottages.

Just to round up the information about the cottages' prostitutes further, Nellie Gaspar had been a circus performer before arriving in New Orleans in 1866. She also worked in the brothel at 111 Dauphine, and was also expelled, mainly for her frequent absences from work, leaving to go out with her boyfriend.

Again, Mr. Asbury tells her tragic story far better than this poor writer could:

> [Nellie] *became an inmate of a Customhouse Street brothel operated by Madame Schneider, who was noted for her bass voice and her demonic temper. Nellie Gaspar's seducer had deserted her and she had taken a new lover. She had been at Madame Schneider's for only a few days when the man who had started her upon the career of a harlot broke into her room, stole all of her money, and beat her unmercifully with the butt of a revolver.*
>
> *She was still alive when found by Madame Schneider, and that big-hearted harridan put her into a small room and traded her water for dresses until her wardrobe was exhausted. Then the girl was sent to Charity Hospital, but was discharged after three days and returned to the brothel in Dauphine Street, where she died within the week.*

The oldest swimming pool in the French Quarter at the Audubon Cottages.

After this unrelenting drama moved on, the cottages reverted back to residential use, undisturbed by unduly bass female voices, Joe the Whipper's noted brawling or feverish bird portraiture. It wasn't until the early 1980s that they were developed as hotel accommodations, originally being an annex of the Maison de Ville at that time. By this time, the neighborhood had changed completely, and the cottages were a much more upscale affair.

In 1991, the cottages were further renovated, revealing the original brick walls and wooden posts. The handmade nails were believed to have come from the Jean Lafitte Blacksmith Shop, though it is debatable if Jean Lafitte, amid his pirating and carousing around every New Orleans bar doing business at the time, had time for any artisanal ironwork.

The Audubon Cottages have been a part of the New Orleans Hotel Collection and were further renovated and reopened in 2012, now forming a high-end, reclusive collection of luxury cottages. A copy of Audubon's book graces each one.

A fountain in the Courtyard of the Audubon Cottages.

Lagniappe

The beautifully ornate swimming pool in the courtyard is said to be the oldest swimming pool in the French Quarter.

The modern-day cottages come with their own butler service.

Cottage three was a particular favorite of Hollywood star Elizabeth Taylor, who would often stay there when she was in town.

Cottages one and seven were used as James Audubon's room and studio respectively.

7.
LE PAVILLON
(FORMERLY THE NEW HOTEL DENECHAUD AND THE HOTEL DESOTO)

The coat check girl is happy with her wages, will not expect a tip and will not so much look at you as if she does.
—*hotel brochure, 1920s*

A few blocks away from the towering pillars that mark the entrance of Le Pavillon Hotel, and across the commercial district of the CBD, lies Orange Street. This nondescript thoroughfare is a lone reminder of the first form of commerce to really exist on these lands, an orange grove that was cultivated and managed by the Catholic Society of Jesuits. That was in the mid-eighteenth century before the area was acquired by Jean Gravier (also immortalized with a nearby street, of course). Thanks in part to him, New Orleans acquired its first suburb: Fauborg St. Marie, later to become the American Sector.

If we skip forward a hundred years, we find that the area had become such a busy hub that the city's very first streetcar was being launched from more or less the very site on which Le Pavillon Hotel now stands, at that time promising easy access to the bright lights and bustling streets of Carrollton.

The economy was robust enough in those days to support a small hotel that had been opened in 1884 by an enterprising youngster called Edward F. Denechaud who was opening his first business, complete with restaurant, at the tender age of nineteen. This opportunistic youngster had come from Bordeaux with his father and had served with the Confederate Guard during the Civil War, after which he stayed on in New Orleans to become an American citizen.

NEW ORLEANS HISTORIC HOTELS

An exterior shot of Le Pavillon Hotel.

His property—the Hotel Denechaud—did brisk trade with its forty-eight rooms, being as it was on the corner of Carondelet and Perdido Streets, just a block away from the prosperous German Theatre (which later became Werlein Hall). Business was good, but the hotel was ultimately ill fated. A gas explosion in 1901 claimed the life of the youngest of Denechaud's children, and by 1910, the hotel was no longer operating and had become the Masonic Temple that still stands there today.

The Denechaud name was far from finished in the New Orleans hotel business, though. In 1904, the Werlein family sold the block of land on which Le Pavillon now stands to developer Émilien Perrin. Perrin was a man of action, evident if nowhere else than in the fact that he had married two sisters and produced nineteen children between them. Between bouts of excessive procreation, he also operated the Equitable Real Estate Company and, with the land secured, set about building a new hotel on Baronne Street. This project was undertaken in tandem with the building of the Civic Theatre, again a testament to Perrin's prolific tendencies.

NEW ORLEANS HISTORIC HOTELS

The year 1907-08 was a big one for New Orleans hotels. The Grunewald and the Monteleone had both expanded, and now this gleaming new property was about to add 250 high-end rooms to the city's rapidly growing portfolio.

Edward Denechaud had more or less retired at this time, though he remained an active and vocal shareholder in Perrin's venture. His son Justin—who had grown up in hotels and been involved in their management for all of his adult life—was recruited to take the helm of this pristine, grand hotel, which was to open under the trusted and by now well-known family name: the New Hotel Denechaud.

The overriding concept for the New Hotel Denechaud could be summed up in a single word: sumptuous. This ran true for all aspects of the building, from the fittings to the architectural work, for which the prestigious local architects Toledano, Wogan and De Buys had been commissioned.

Modern Renaissance and French Renaissance were both styles that were bandied about to describe the overall look, both being an acceptable interpretation of the resplendent building that was erected. There was a dazzling combination of white floors hewn from Italian marble, huge marble columns and pilasters and decadent mahoganies and bronzes festooning the public spaces. Even the rooms boasted a marble ceramic that immediately placed the hotel's accommodations in the upper echelons of the burgeoning local hospitality industry.

Technical flourishes abounded, and were—for the time—extremely expensive and impressive. The hotel installed the city's first hydraulic-plunger elevators, sophisticated soundproofing techniques were applied to the walls between the rooms and state-of-the-art air filtering mechanisms were painstakingly fitted. Sensitive to the inferno that had brought tragedy to the Denechaud family in their first hotel, the building's designers planned a vast system of water pumps in the basement, and the hotel—built as it was, mainly from steel and concrete—was essentially fireproof.

On January 14, 1907, the hotel opened with a show of florid opulence: a champagne bottle was smashed on the marble floor of the lobby as a way of christening this gleaming testament to an affluent future. The local press described the entire scene as something akin to a breathtaking botanical garden, and a shy Justin Denechaud made a brief but proud speech.

This impressive new hotel was advertised nationwide, its fireproof construction high up on the list of amenities, as well as boasts of the finest orchestra in the South. Room rates started out at $1.50 a night.

The Café le Gallerie, which was part of the New Hotel Denechaud.

It was a confident opening, but sadly for Justin Denechaud and despite the pomp and ceremony, this incarnation of the hotel was not to be the success that the cartel of investors had hoped for. The draw of the family name had been overestimated, and running costs had been wildly underestimated. On June 2, 1910, the board changed, as did the hotel's name. Justin Denechaud was reluctantly dismissed, and Émilien Perrin took time out from his furtherance of the species to step up and manage what had become the Hotel DeSoto.

Boardroom deals and a series of liquidations and investments marked the early years of the Hotel DeSoto, with money coming in from Texas to ease the strains of the Great Depression, some of it from a thrusting hotelier and entrepreneur by the name of Conrad Hilton.

As the 1920s advanced, the hotel held its place in the city directory and had a prominent place among only eleven listed hotels. The hotel ran advertising campaigns that effusively boasted about the "elbow room" of the accommodations and the rarefied atmosphere, which was nebulously defined as "tone without glare." A glare-less room that could maintain its tone at this time cost around three dollars a night.

The hotel was also keen to push the restaurant and introduced sixty-cent lunches and dollar dinner menus under the auspices of Chef Maximillian Richter. One hotel brochure assures its more thrifty guests that they needn't worry about tipping the coat check girl and with little tact explains that "she is happy with her wages, will not expect a tip and will not so much look at you as if she does." One can only imagine the directions given to the poor girl on how to manage her facial expressions.

In the same brochure, Chef Richter somewhat needily makes his case: "I am considered in New Orleans, rather good at the dishes called 'Southern Cookery' most particularly. I would like you, Sir or Madam, to prove whether I deserve such a reputation." Obligating diners to prove something as a means of drumming up business was a strange tactic, but it seemed to work, for a while at least.

Of course, at this time, radio was growing rapidly as a medium, and the station WDSU—one of six stations in the city—began broadcasting from the top floor of the DeSoto in 1928. The hotel became a hub for an unlikely pioneer within the field of mass media. WDSU broadcast the first prizefight and football game in the United States and was the first station to broadcast from an airplane. WDSU grew quickly and would, in 1948, expand to become the city's first TV station.

Unsurprisingly, local politicians were keen to usurp the airways, and the governor, senator and notorious self-publicist Huey P. Long would make regular departures from his home at the Roosevelt Hotel to set up operations on the top floor for one of his marathon broadcasts.

Long was a famously provocative and divisive character, even pushing people to behavioral extremes, as his assassination in 1935 tragically proves. In June of that year, the Long camp had allegedly learned from a spy of theirs that a plot to kill Long was being discussed at the Democratic Conference, which was taking place that year at the DeSoto.

The surveillance operation would seem almost comic if it weren't for the fatal consequences. Long's aides had planted a staff member of theirs as a hotel insider, setting him up with a job as a desk clerk. This helped them gain access to all the rooms, and they were easily able to smuggle their people into suites neighboring the room where the suspected meeting was to take place.

Using a long pole and a recording device, Long's people snooped on the assassination plot, which they suspected was being hatched by New Orleans mayor Semmes Walmsley, various other high-ranking politicians and Dr. Carl Weiss, Huey Long's eventual assassin. The hotel was thrust into a controversial limelight as the transcript was made public by Long

The Dining Room of the DeSoto Hotel.

the next day. Long was shot dead by Carl Weiss in Baton Rouge just thirty-six hours later.

The next thirty years sadly saw a gradual decline in the Hotel DeSoto's levels of sophistication and elegance. Elaborate furnishings and luxurious touches were slowly withdrawn or not replaced, and by the late 1950s, architectural remainders of the hotel's grand opening and astonishing appearance were few and far between. A couple of Art Deco details remained, but the hotel was not the grand building it had once been.

In 1963, the Hotel DeSoto Company was liquidated. The property lay dormant until 1971, when a local business partnership bought the hotel for $800,000 and secured a $6 million investment to go to work on the still solid foundations (testament to the fine architectural work by the original builders) and restore the building to its former greatness.

Headed by local hotelier Gerald Senner, the team went to work, striving to reconfigure the original French flourishes and renaming the hotel Le Pavillon—in translation "the Pavillion"—a name which the parties involved felt encapsulated their lofty ideals and ambition.

Architect James Gibert was enlisted to realize the vision, design the rooms and, most importantly, create and add the opulent frontage of the hotel that is to this day such a remarkable part of the building's aesthetic.

The renaissance of the hotel was all encompassing. Interior designers traveled to Italy and France to collect artifacts and furnishings; Spanish ironwork was collected; new suites and a swimming pool were added; and the grand columns and gaslight (the largest one of its kind in America) of the entrance were confidently foisted onto the Poydras Street streetscape.

The bar was again fitted with mahogany, replacing the seedy remains of the 1950s, and marble balustrades were erected, complemented with green onyx. Fine artworks—some sixteen paintings for every floor of the hotel—were later purchased and assembled as a collection, including locally famous works, such as the nineteenth-century portrait *The Belle of New Orleans*, which hangs in the Crystal Room. This portrait is particularly appropriate as this was the nickname that the hotel would strive to work into the marketing campaigns of its early days.

The new Le Pavillon Hotel opened its doors in 1971, and its grand character and plush interiors would certainly have pleased the Denechaud family and, one suspects, even the panoramic appetites of Émilien Perrin. From the fifteen-foot monumental limestone statues of the entranceway ("Peace" and "Prosperity") to the rare, three-arch Brunswick Bar, the high ideals of the builders of the New Denechaud Hotel were met, and the hotel continues to be a bastion of period beauty.

Lagniappe

On June 24, 1991, Le Pavillon was placed on the National Register of Historic Places by the U.S. Department of the Interior.

Each evening at 10:00 p.m., the hotel serves a complimentary supper feast of peanut butter and jelly sandwiches to its guests, along with ice-cold milk and hot chocolate. This tradition was started in 1988, when a traveling salesman ordered this very thing at the bar as a symbol of sharing in his daughter's supper even though she was at home, many miles away. The bartender that night was by chance the general manager of the hotel, and as fellow bar guests began to notice and ordered the same thing, the manager was so touched that he decided to make it a nightly service.

Although Louis Armstrong never did grace the hotel with his trumpet playing, his mother, Mary Ann, worked at the hotel as a maid and his stepfather, Tom, worked as a waiter.

The hotel owns a marble bathtub, hand carved from a single block of Carrara marble, which is said to have belonged to Napoleon Bonaparte himself. Only three of these tubs exist in the world: one in a private collection, one in the Louvre in Paris and one in the collection of Le Pavillon Hotel.

Most of the hotel's reported ghostly presences seem to predate even the DeSoto age of the building. A spectral girl has been spotted, reportedly the spirit of a young woman who was mown down by a horse and carriage outside the hotel. Staff and guests also tell of a well-dressed young man in nineteenth-century regalia that plays pranks and disappears. A visiting doctor also checked out after waking to see a gray-haired old woman at his bedside. Morgan Murphy, a writer for *Southern Living* magazine, reported his door creaking "like a bad Vincent Price movie," so it's best to avoid Room 301 if you're wary of that sort of thing.

8.
OMNI ROYAL ORLEANS
(FORMERLY THE CITY EXCHANGE, THE ST. LOUIS HOTEL, THE ROYAL ORLEANS HOTEL)

The dome of this building is very fine and richly frescoed. It is adorned with allegorical pictures and busts of famous men, the work of Canova and Pinoli. This building was originally the Bourse of the city, and a fine hotel was combined with it.
—Lafcadio Hearn, 1885

If war is the mother of invention, then civic rivalry is the mother of construction, and it was the appearance in the American Sector of the St. Charles Hotel, which started to rise up in 1835, that spurred a suitably grand reply from the European side of New Orleans.

From the French side of Canal Street, one Jacques Nicolas Bussiere DePoilly looked sniffily on at the grandeur being erected across the way and decided to retaliate by building a hotel that Creole society could be proud of. Sure, DePoilly wanted a testament to beauty on its own merits, but sticking one to the Americans and their hoity-toity hotel was definitely a satisfying slice of lagniappe.

By 1836, DePoilly, backed by money from his associate Pierre Soulé, had signed contracts, and work began on his grand scheme. The details of the contract spoke grandly of geometric perfection and cypress woods of unsurpassable quality, but the underlying object was more prosaic: be a better hotel than the St. Charles.

The grand lobby of the Omni Royal Hotel.

DePoilly and his corporation (the somewhat dramatically named Company of Amelioration) envisioned a place of culture, of commerce and of class, and he wanted it to take up the entire block formed by the streets of Royal, Toulouse, Chartres and St. Louis.

The block was already a bustling center of Creole life, being home to La Bourse de Maspero, also known as Maspero's Exchange. Redoubtable owner Pierre Maspero had long served up coffee and liquor to the city's merchants, and his large café and barroom was routinely awash with businessmen and local journalists. General Andrew Jackson was certainly a regular, and if his Battle of New Orleans plans were not actually drawn up in Maspero's, then the discussions leading up to them certainly took place there.

In 1838, the café was taken over by entrepreneur James Hewlett, who, with questionable taste, immediately introduced a billiards, cockfighting and beer-only bar. The place was swallowed up and leveled to fit DePoilly's creation, which, despite its grand intentions (looking to emulate the Rue de Rivoli in Paris), met with unfortunate timing: a financial crisis in 1837 meant that plans were scaled back.

Nevertheless, an impressive edifice presented itself to Creole society in May 1838. A huge vestibule loomed over the St. Louis side, leading into a decorous bar, plush ballrooms and a second entrance on Royal Street. Above these gleaming public spaces sat enough rooms to welcome six hundred guests.

The highlight, though, sat where Maspero (who had been reinstated to manage the new space) and Hewlett had had their exchanges: the City Exchange, a cavernous rotunda and the principle arena for commerce in New Orleans.

The most famous and oft-quoted report of walking through the rotunda came from George Buckingham soon after, in 1842, when the place was at full throttle:

> [The auctioneer was] *endeavouring to drown* [out] *every voice but his own. One was selling pictures and dwelling on their merits; another was disposing of some slaves. These consisted of an unhappy family who were all exposed to the hammer at the same time. Their good qualities were enumerated in English and in French, and their persons were carefully examined by intending purchasers, among whom they were ultimately disposed of, chiefly to Creole buyers; the husband at 750 dollars, the wife at 550, and the children at 220 each.*

Maspero was ably assisted in his hosting duties by a cook named Alvarez. Accounts attribute Alvarez with the invention (though more likely it was the popularization) of gumbo, though he more certainly pioneered the free lunches that, within years, had become a staple of high-class bars the country over. In any case, by 1840, Alvarez had replaced Maspero as manager of the exchange. Joseph Santini took up Alvarez's post, a position that obviously came with added inspiration as he in turn invented two beloved mixed drinks, the Crusta and Santini's Pousse-Café.

It was around this time that the building was—in even more belligerent defiance of American sensibilities—becoming known as the St. Louis. The rotunda drew such attention that it is said to be the inspiration for scenes in Harriet Beecher Stowe's 1852 novel, *Uncle Tom's Cabin*, in which she imagined a New Orleans hotel rotunda where Uncle Tom and his fellow slaves were sold.

As was the fate of many a building at the time, fire beset the place in 1841. These things were taken stoically, though, and reassuringly, the St. Charles would undergo the same fate more than once. Rather than spelling the end of DePoilly's dream, his plans were dusted off, and after some speedy reconstruction (if expensive—some reports put the cost at $600,000), the rebirth actually ushered in the beginning of what was to become the hotel's golden age.

As strange at it seemed to enlist the services of a purveyor of billiards and cockfighting, James Hewlett was bought in to replace Alvarez as manager, and despite his low-life past, Helwett actually managed to launch the St. Louis into a social stratosphere that was previously unimaginable.

He did this with a pincer movement of social occasions. He initiated the throwing of incredibly lavish balls and banquets that drew envious eyes, even from the famously hard-to-impress socialites of New York and Boston.

One of the most famous and widely reported banquets was that to entertain the politician Henry Clay. The French Opera House Company were brought in to perform musical duties, and a dinner seat would cost you $100—a not insubstantial ticket price even by today's standards. Six hundred people were apparently wealthy enough to attend, though, and the $60,000 payday was a triumph. Hewlett also quickly lured in the revelries of the Mystic Krewe of Comus, cementing the hotel's associations with the already large-scale (and big-spending) pageantry of Mardi Gras.

The Omni Royal's private dining room, called the Escoffier.

These sweet times would soon sour, though, and while Henry Clay's efforts to focus on diplomacy between North and South were commendable, the cheers around him in the dining room of the St. Louis Hotel would soon be no more than dead echoes. The party was quickly coming to an end.

New Orleans's experience of the Civil War is a vastly complicated and wide-ranging subject, but suffice it to say that with regard to the history of this one hotel, a celebratory, hedonistic way of life was cleaved and rendered to no more than a memory over the following years.

The St. Louis Hotel had grandstand seats to the conflict, not least because in 1874, after a succession of owners, the building was sold to the state of Louisiana for $235,000. It was a combative, confrontational period for the region and for the hotel in particular, especially as it was actively used as the seat of Louisiana government on several occasions between 1874 and 1877.

It was around this time that the proto-travel journalist Lafcadio Hearn was writing essays on New Orleans for the *Daily City Item*, and in one such report, he felt moved to mention the hotel: "The old St. Louis Hotel, on St. Louis, Chartres and Royal streets, should also be visited. The dome of this building is very fine and richly frescoed. It is adorned with allegorical pictures and busts of famous men, the work of Canova and Pinoli. This building was originally the Bourse of the city, and a fine hotel was combined with it."

The building was witness to myriad political and social uprisings, and as Louisiana's Reconstruction came to an end, things looked bleak. The hotel opened its doors to house returning Confederate soldiers, revenues fell and its place as the height of society was a scarcely remembered dream.

The St. Louis would continue to exist—a shell of its former self—for around forty more years. Optimistic reopenings and refurbishments were a perennial occurrence, though the advertising copy became less and less alluring and the language more and more uninspiring. "The terms are as reasonable as even the most economical could expect," ran one rather uninspiring line, hardly an exciting invitation to the banquet of the century.

In 1884, the government leased the hotel to a man called R.J. Rivers, and though he renamed the property, running it as the Hotel Royal and making what renovations he reasonably could, it was hard to shake the reputation that had been attached to the St. Louis—that of a fallen giant that had seen much better days.

Times were changing, new hotels were springing up and, in an insult to DePoilly and Soulé, people just unquestioningly preferred the St. Charles. Restaurants were becoming popular, meaning that people no longer relied on hotels to eat out. The Creole population no longer had their shining beacon—it had been taken from them like "a dishonest waiter stealing one silver knife or fork at a time," as John DeMers so beautifully puts it in his book *The Tumultuous Life and Times of the Omni Royal Orleans Hotel*.

Rivers gave up the lease, the government sold the property off and the building lay derelict. In another oft-quoted incident that sums up the poignant feelings of disappointment, the writer John Galsworthy recalled a visit to New Orleans in 1912. He had been taken into the old hotel (tours were being given for twenty-five cents) to view the rotunda and the slave auction block. His guide was an old Creole woman who opined: "Yes, sir. Here they all came. 'Twas the finest hotel, before the war-time…all the old Southern families, buyin' an' sellin' their property."

Galsworthy, in his book *The Inn of Tranquility*, goes on to recall "the dark, denuded dankness of that old hotel, rotting with damp and time." Just in case there was any confusion, his wife, Ada, added, "For gruesome, unfaked melancholy, I've never seen anything like it." So, we can reasonably assume, it was not the cheeriest of spots in the city to pay a visit to.

Ada Galsworthy hadn't seen anything yet, though. In 1915, the building was condemned as a hazard connected with a bubonic plague outbreak, but apparently even man-handled demolition was too honorable a fate, as that year's hurricane all but leveled the former site of the great Creole hope.

A lumberyard and a small praline shop were the relatively ignominious businesses to occupy what for some decades was really an undesirable plot of real estate in the French Quarter. The American Sector had won out with its far-reaching vision, and the French Quarter occupied a lowly place, with no real construction and certainly no wealthy investors looking to construct large hotels.

So it may have come to a surprise to many in June 1957 when local newspapers ran with a story about a new, $6 million hotel being slated to open right on the spot where the City Exchange once stood. Local entrepreneur and philanthropist Edgar Stern, with fellow businessman Lester Kabacoff, saw the potential, and after unsuccessfully showing the site to Conrad Hilton and the Sheraton company, a new property was envisioned.

All interested parties agreed that the hotel had to reflect the grandeur of its past incarnation, to honor the memories that some people had of that spot, and with the help of architects Arthur Q. Davis and Samuel Davis Jr., plans for a hotel that Davis described as "reminiscent of the Georges V or Ritz in Paris" were submitted to the Vieux Carré commission.

As the hotel reports:

The famous Omni Royal Rib Room.

> *The hotel was constructed to exacting specifications set forth by the Vieux Carré Commission which oversee all historic preservation efforts in the French Quarter. It was to be built upon exact drawing of the St. Louis Hotel with its famed arches, Spanish wrought iron railings down to the precise height and dimensions which outlined the Paris look Mansard Roof.*

One of the most difficult decisions, along with all the interior and exterior design plans, was the nature of the flagship restaurant. It had long been intended that the hotel should trumpet a Creole restaurant of the highest caliber, but when research showed that several high-class Creole restaurants were in fact within a stone's throw of the hotel, it was time for a rethink.

The Rib Room would be a restaurant specializing in prime beef, a very British addition to the French Quarter dining scene, but one that proved so successful that it not only eventually cemented the hotel's culinary reputation in town but also provided a model for many of the hotel company's other openings.

A hotel worthy of DePoilly's vision was built up from the rubble, even including his precious cypress wood as a major constituent of the interior. The Royal Orleans Hotel, after the usual forays into the bureaucratic battleground that surrounds construction in the French Quarter, had its gala opening on October 8, 1960.

Battling for business and going up against the fame of the Roosevelt and the Monteleone, the hotel had to employ innovative tactics—it was the first hotel to advertise on billboards on the road from the airport, for example. But this steeliness, perhaps borne from the adversarial spirit of the original City Exchange, has seen it flourish and become a French Quarter institution in its own right, through its acquisition and rebranding by Omni and up to modern times.

Lagniappe

In 1970, Jazz Fest was celebrating its inaugural year, and Louis Armstrong was in town as a guest. The Royal Orleans had a ball in his honor with the Preservation Hall band and an award presented to him from the governor of Louisiana. It proved to be his last hometown appearance, as he died the following year.

For a long time, the Royal Orleans had a doorman, John, who was seven feet, eight inches tall.

Famous names that have stayed include Michael Jackson, the Rolling Stones, Zsa Zsa Gabor, Paul Newman, Richard Nixon and the king of Norway.

The restaurant the Original Pierre Maspero's stands at 440 Chartres Street to this day, the sign reading, "Established 1788."

The Rib Room was originally a male-only restaurant. To this day, there is only a men's bathroom. Martin Girls would make and serve cocktails to guests right at their table using a drinks trolley on wheels. The hotel boasts that "the idea for Superdome and the Louisiana Jazz and Heritage Festival were developed in the Pipkin Room within the restaurant."

The book (and subsequent film and TV show) *Hotel* by Arthur Hailey was largely influenced by the author's observations about life in the Royal Orleans. A particularly appropriate exchange has the protagonist saying, "There are some people who believe that the Royal Orleans is the finest hotel in North America. Whether you agree or not doesn't matter much. The point is: it shows how good a hotel can be."

The large plate mirrors in the main dining room at Antoine's Restaurant were formerly found in the Grand Ballrooms of the St. Louis, imported from France.

9.
SONIAT HOUSE

The house was reputed to have been filled with lovely things.
—Martha Ann Samuels

The somewhat nondescript front door on the 1100 block of Decatur hides one of the city's most discreet luxury hotels. The architecture and interiors are a handy visual metaphor for the city's ethnography and history—Creole and American touches, Georgian and French flourishes.

The building dates back to around 1829, when it was built for Joseph Soniat du Fossat. Joseph was the son of the Chevalier Guy Saunhac du Fossat, who had arrived in Louisiana in 1751 and had immediately increased his stock as a military engineer, helping quell Indian uprisings and being decorated for his efforts.

Guy married above himself (please, no old jokes about how "all men do")—to a relative of King Louis VI of France, no less—so young Joseph had at least a smattering of royal blood in his veins. He wasted little time in extending this pseudo-royal family line, siring four sons with his first wife, Marie Ann Arnoult, before she died.

His second wife, Louise Duralde, was from a suitably high family, and she and her two sisters were local New Orleans legends, each apparently boasting the killer combination of beauty, grace and political wit. Her beauty especially must have been particularly irresistible as Joseph and Louise added nine more children to the Soniat line. At this time, they lived

A modern-day exterior shot of the Soniat House.

in an opulent plantation some distance away, a building which eventually became the clubhouse of the Colonial Country Club in Harahan.

The need for a large house in town coincided with the sale of 1135 Chartres Street by the Ursuline nuns, who owned quite the portfolio of property in this corner of the French Quarter. The Soniat family bought the house in 1828 for $3,262, and in 1829, the builder François Boisdore began work to transform the property.

It's clear that a hotel-sized property was needed for a family that includes thirteen children and all the entourage of in-laws, grandchildren, etc., and the expansive house was opened up into the backs of neighboring houses, where Madame Soniat's sisters conveniently lived, making the block a cornerstone of New Orleans high society.

In her essay on the property, "Creole-American Blend Seen in This Fine Home," Martha Ann Samuels notes the probable beauty inside the house at that time: "The house was reputed to have been filled with lovely things; great half-tester beds of rosewood and mahogany, magnificent armoires, dressers and doubtless a duchesse, sofas of acajou and damask, marble-topped tables, all the richly carved work of the New Orleans masters like Selgnouret, Mallard, and Selbrecht."

One of the suites at the Soniat House.

She also notes the aesthetic allure displayed by the property's residents: "Like all the women of this time, Mme. Soniat was said to have had an exquisite skin, and according to the family she never appeared in the harsh light of the courtyard without a bonnet and a heavy blue veil to shield her beauty."

Out in the courtyard—the buildings that now provide accommodations for the hotel's discerning guests, there is a two-story slave quarter building of orange brick and a wooden gallery. This would have been the original kitchen, workrooms and quarters for the servants. Also back here were all the other small outbuildings of the time, probably built as a miniature replication of the plantation that Joseph had moved from.

Joseph Soniat enjoyed just over twenty years in this idyllic home until he died in 1852, though Madame Soniat lived on there until 1865. The house was sold to a Pablo Gelpi, who for an obviously wealthy individual there is very little information. We do know that he was responsible for the ripping off of the old wrought iron railings and cornice and adding the extensive gallery you see today, as was the fashion of the times.

The house went through a succession of owners after this period, all while this neighborhood became less and less salubrious, something no doubt reflected in the state of the property. The dilapidation found by

A member of the staff serving breakfast at the Soniat House.

buyer Nathaniel Felton in 1945 was notable, and it was here that the careful restoration that pays such dividends today started out.

The Soniat House of today opened its doors as a hotel in 1984. It remains one of the most atmospheric and well-maintained properties in the Quarter, and there's little beyond that plain front door to suggest anything has changed since those days in the 1830s. This is true right down to the breakfasts of homemade preserves and biscuits, heated on hot flat stones, as must have been brought to Joseph Soniat a century and a half ago.

Lagniappe

The hotel has a public lounge with an honesty bar. You can pour your own cocktail and then simply charge yourself.

The famous biscuits are made fresh each day and served with freshly squeezed orange juice.

The hotel owns a suite-filled annex right across the road.

The hotel is a favorite of rock stars Michael Stipe and Patti Smith, as well as actor John Malkovich.

Soniat House has to be one of the few hotels in the French Quarter *not* to be haunted—or at least one of the few that doesn't publicize it.

10.
THE MONTELEONE

More than a landmark, the heart of New Orleans.
—Jenny Adams

Together with the Roosevelt and Le Pavillon, this colorfully charismatic hotel, brimming with stories and gossip and literature and cocktails, forms the trio of the oldest continually operating hotels in the city. Yes, the Roosevelt Hotel closed for a time after Hurricane Katrina, but if we're being generous with our classification, and there's little reason not to be, then these are the properties that have weathered the demands of New Orleans life.

The Hotel Monteleone is one of the last, classic, family-owned hotels in America, having been operated by four generations of the Monteleone family over the past century. In many ways, it is a modern day success story and it encapsulates the optimism of nineteenth-century immigration to the city.

In the mid-1800s, this block of Royal Street was fairly nondescript, being made up largely of private residences and assorted boardinghouses. The atmosphere perked up considerably when, in 1883, the Park Theatre opened its doors. An advertisement in the *Daily States* from September 24, 1883, announced its arrival: "Park Theatre, Royal Street will open Saturday, September 29, with Harry Guion's greatest of all Female Minstrel Combinations to be followed in rapid succession by other star companies."

Show business continued apace, and the building became the Eden Theatre in 1886, opening with a free ticket to anyone who cared to come see the new, improved facility. An editorial in the September 18, 1886 *Mascot*

A modern-day exterior shot of the Hotel Monteleone.

outlines the joys which await, promising a particular treat for those people who were fans of male waiters:

> The auditorium and stage proper will take up the whole of the lower floor which, with proscenium boxes, and dress circle gallery above, gives a seating capacity of 1,500 persons. On the second floor are the Grand Café, salons and promenades, all gorgeously decorated and embellished with works of art, beds and urns of natural flowers and other ornaments. The floors are fully carpeted and matted and the distribution of chairs, tables and private parlors so arranged as to afford the best opportunity for obtaining a measurable secrecy from view, while enjoying the performance on the stage.
>
> The sideboards will be supplied with a full assortment of the very best brands and makes of wines, liquors. A full corps of male waiters, well trained and coached, will be employed, no female waiters will be employed in or about the establishment. Among the first attractions which will be produced will be The Great French Burlesque Opera Troupe. The Grand Opening will take place on Saturday evening, Sept. 18, 1886 at 7:30 to which the public is invited gratis.

Antonio Monteleone had arrived from Sicily in the early 1880s and worked in a cobbler and shoe store owned by his uncle Richard located across from the theater. He immediately gained respectability due to his craftsmanship and work ethic and expanded the business to new buildings on the corner of St. Louis and Royal Streets and to another location at Royal and Conti Streets.

It didn't take long for the lure of the American dream to shape Antonio's ambition, and he began to buy land, first on Decatur Street and followed by lots on St. Philip. In 1886, he purchased the building at 54 Royal Street, the lot adjacent to the current site of the hotel. It became the family home for him and his wife, Sophia, and their children.

Antonio began to diversify his business interests, opening up a small, three-story hotel on the corner of Iberville and Royal Streets, and by 1894, he was listed in the city directory as a hotel proprietor. By 1898, he was able to expand the town house–hotel, developing it into a five-story concern. At this time, he had also invested in yet more property and was the landlord of the Hotel Victor, also on this block, which changed its name to the Commercial Hotel just before the turn of the century.

Advertisements ran in local newspapers around that time, announcing the new incarnation of the Commercial Hotel. Rooms started at a dollar a

A portrait of Antonio Monteleone.

night, already challenging the Royal and the Grunewald on price, a sign of Antonio's long-term intentions. They may well have sat up and paid attention, for the future came pretty quickly.

With the help of a trusted associate, James Kenney, the vision of a single hotel building incorporating Antonio's house and the Commercial Hotel became a meaningful possibility. Lot by lot, Antonio bought his way around the block, seeing off the vaudeville types he thought of as seedy, and a contractor, George Glover, was enlisted to build what would become the original Hotel Monteleone.

Indoors, luxurious touches were slowly but surely being added to the Commercial Hotel, again a foreshadowing of Monteleone's ambition.

Private bubble baths and grand chandeliers sprang up, the freshest seafood available was promised and—invisible but just as important—state-of-the-art safety measures were installed.

Work began feverishly on a Louis XIV– or French Renaissance–style property, replete with grand staircase, elevators, wooden carvings in the public spaces and 220 rooms, 160 of which had baths and all of which had electric lights. The hotel was successfully fireproofed, and in 1908, the first guests checked into a major new addition to the city's hotel portfolio.

The hotel was an immediate success. Antonio won himself favor with all who worked for him, advocating union labor and averting a number of crises—a man of the people who could also mix in the high-society circles that hotel ownership demanded. It was an elegant and fashionable block with the theaters nearby, Galpin's restaurant (which had opened in 1861) and various private clubs, including the Shakespeare Club and the Germania Club.

The period 1907–08 was era-defining for the New Orleans hotel industry, this also being when the Jung Hotel opened on Canal Street, the New Hotel Denechaud opened on Poydras and the Grunewald also underwent a major expansion.

Tragically, Antonio Monteleone died in 1913. He was only fifty-eight years old and was traveling in Germany at the time. Newspaper reports recall how distressing the news was to his hotel staff and to all who knew him, which was an impressively large slice of the city. The hotel passed to his son, Frank, who, being so young, ran the hotel with Kenney, who had himself married into the family by that time, having wed Stella Monteleone. It's worth noting that in 1926, room prices still started at one dollar a night, even amid the relative luxury.

This new team oversaw the addition of the Queen Anne Ballroom and two hundred more rooms in 1928, a year before the Great Depression. This economic crash should have been a death knell for a large hotel with high overheads such as the Monteleone, but somehow the hotel not only survived but also remained in the ownership of the Monteleone family, a rare and laudable occurrence during these lean times.

The *New Orleans City Guide* of 1938 lists these amenities in the hotel at the time, when basic room prices had risen a whole fifty cents: "Monteleone Hotel, 214 Royal St.; 600 rooms 540 have radios, 500 have private baths, and all have hot and cold running water and ceiling fans; rates $1.50–$3.50. European plan; garage 50c, parking lot 15c; convention hall, dining-room, coffee shop, bar, and beauty parlor."

The Carousel Bar at the Hotel Monteleone, 1960s.

America emerged from the Depression, and the big band era ushered in a new time of optimism. By 1938, the radio station WDSU had also set up shop in one of the rooms, as noted in the 1938 *New Orleans City Guide*:

> *WDSU, studios at 1456 Monteleone Hotel, 214 Royal St. (open daily 8A.M.-10P.M.; free), broadcasts on an assigned frequency of 1220 kilocycles with a power of 1000 watts. Programs of the N.B.C.'s Blue Network and electrical transcriptions of the World Broadcasting System are presented from 7 A.M. to midnight. Broadcasting of "Pelican" ball games and other local events are featured.*

By 1949, the hotel's lounge, the Swan Room, was a fashionable music venue, and Frank Monteleone had matured into a sophisticated host and hotelier, welcoming stars such as Robert Mitchum into the hotel and being photographed with the great and the good of the day.

The hotel was then about to transform one of the present-day hotel's most cherished spots. The Carousel Piano Bar & Lounge is the only revolving bar in New Orleans, a twenty-five-seat carousel (installed in 1949) that turns on two thousand large steel rollers, pulled by a chain powered by a one-quarter horsepower motor at a constant rate of one revolution every fifteen minutes. In the 1950s and 1960s, this weird rotating bar and its attendant supper club were without competition in terms of sheer novelty, and the venue claimed Liberace, Etta James and Louis Prima as performers. It was high times for the Hotel Monteleone, Antonio's dreams truly realized.

In 1954, the hotel saw its last major redevelopment, an almost total demolition and overhaul that resulted in the grand property of today, with its ballrooms, meeting facilities and the bars and restaurants that you can now visit. It became the only real high-rise building in the French Quarter at the time, which was not a universally popular move, the *Times-Picayune* reporting protests by local business and homeowners.

By 1964, however, the hotel was already boasting its penthouse space and Sky Terrace, an extra two-story structure on the existing building that also included a Presidential Suite for visiting dignitaries and a rooftop putting green for hotel guests.

The hotel had by now built up a reputation as a literary hangout, with noted social butterflies (for which read functioning and very talented drunks) Truman Capote, Eudora Welty, William Faulkner and Tennessee Williams all frequent guests.

According to hotel historian Charlie Farrae (you can read a full interview with him in Appendix I), Hemingway's short story "Night Before Battle" was penned during a stay at the Monteleone. Williams mentions the hotel in *The Rose Tattoo*, and the hotel is awash with fans when the annual Tennessee Williams Festival rolls into the city. A display case in the lobby shows off various literary artifacts.

Frank Monteleone died in 1958, and the hotel passed on to his son and Antonio's grandson, William, affectionately known as Billy. The 1960s were a particularly challenging time for the hotel, competing as it was with not only a rash of new hotels opening up across the city but also hotels directly impinging on its market—the Omni Royal was suddenly taking most of the celebrity business, for example.

The consistency of the family ownership, a commitment to tradition and taking a chance on Old World charm as opposed to going up against the Sheratons and Marriotts that arrived in the 1980s seem to have paid dividends. The long-serving staff all speak highly of the generosity of the family (again, see the interview with Charlie Farrae), and the Monteleone still manages to stand out in an increasingly crowded market place.

The Eudora Welty room at the Hotel Monteleone.

In 2011, the fourth generation of Monteleones took over the running of this great New Orleans institution as Billy Monteleone passed away and his son William Jr., one of the great-grandsons of a cobbler named Antonio Monteleone, was handed the baton. The famed grandfather clock still chimes in the lobby, the doormen still hail taxis and hold doors for luggage-laden arrivals and the Carousel Bar still revolves every fifteen minutes.

Lagniappe

For more on the life and works of Antonio Monteleone, and for lots of context about the life and times of the hotel, I thoroughly recommend *Hotel Monteleone: More Than a Landmark, the Heart of New Orleans* by Jenny Adams.

As noted, numerous authors were frequent visitors and the hotel has often appeared as a setting in American fiction, prompting the Friends of Libraries USA to designate Hotel Monteleone a Literary Landmark.

Tennessee Williams often claimed he was conceived at the hotel. Truman Capote claimed he was born in the hotel, though the hotel states that he wasn't and that although his mother lived at the hotel during her pregnancy, she safely made it to the hospital in time for Truman's birth.

Anne Rice, Stephen Ambrose and John Grisham have also joined the ranks of literary guests over the years.

The full list of the Monteleone's literary references is *The Rose Tattoo* and *Orpheus Rising* (Tennessee Williams), *Divine Secrets of the Ya-Ya Sisterhood* and *Little Altars Everywhere* (Rebecca Wells), *Band of Brothers* (Stephen Ambrose), *A Piece of My Heart* (Richard Ford), *A Curtain of Green* (Eudora Welty), *Owls Don't Blink* (Stanley Gardner), *Night Before Battle* (Ernest Hemingway) and *The Voice of Seven Sparrows* (Harry Stephen Keeler).

The hotel has been the backdrop to a number of films: *Double Jeopardy* (1999), *Glory Road* (2004), *The Last Time* (2005), *Retirement* (2005) and *12 Rounds* (2008) among them.

11.
THE CORNSTALK HOTEL

Hey, honey, I saw this beautiful cornstalk fence uptown today...
—*Unnamed wife of an Iowan businessman...possibly*

If you're driving or biking down Royal Street, chances are you will see a gaggle of people taking photos of this Victorian building or a mule buggy stopped outside while the driver points out the ironwork on this quirky property.

It's an impressive-looking home, set tastefully back from the street and with a huge front porch, where usually, a couple of smug-looking guests are sitting back with ice tea or Pimm's cups as you walk past, sweltering and wishing you, too, were on vacation, sipping cocktails.

The building's grandeur attracted high-profile owners, even as far back as the early 1800s, when Judge François Xavier Martin lived there. This accomplished fellow was not only the chief justice of the Louisiana Supreme Court at the time but also the author of the first history of Louisiana.

Martin had been appointed attorney general of the territory of Orleans just after the Louisiana Purchase and was responsible for the undoubtedly thankless task of helping to untangle the complicated layers of French and Spanish colonial law. As such, he was well placed to write authoritatively on the subject of New Orleans and published his best-known work, *The History of Louisiana from the Earliest Period*, which appeared in two volumes over the years 1827 to 1829.

Coming back to those tourists, snapping photos and hearing tales in their buggy tour, what they're looking at and hearing about is the iron fence out

An exterior shot of the Cornstalk Hotel.

front, which depicts rows of—perhaps you can hazard a guess here—yes, corn stalks. Every guided tour that passes by here relates the same tale: around 150 years ago, the house was owned by an Iowan businessman, who had brought with him his homesick wife to live in New Orleans.

To appease her, the story goes, he commissioned the fence so that as she looked out of the parlor window, she might have a constant reminder of her home state. It's a heartwarming tale, though possibly apocryphal.

NEW ORLEANS HISTORIC HOTELS

It's an obvious point, but the corn stalks have been rendered on the outside of the iron fence. Impressive and whimsical as they are, they are in a great place for passing visitors to take photos of, but not in a great place for homesick wives to gaze at, teary-eyed, from their front windows.

Secondly, there's the inconvenient coincidence that an almost identical fence can be found uptown surrounding the equally decorous home of Colonel Robert Henry Short. Although there is no proof that the fences come from the same ironworks, the much more likely explanation is probably that the Iowan's wife saw the wonderful fence as she passed by the colonel's villa one day and asked her husband to buy one for her, too.

You can annoy tourists and all tour guides by repeating this theory whenever you hear them starting out with their version—assuming you don't have better things to do, of course.

The building also has a literary connection as it hosted Harriet Beecher Stowe, who was apparently inspired to write her novel *Uncle Tom's Cabin* from the sights she witnessed at the nearby slave markets.

The present-day property has been a hotel since 1961, and retains its eclectic Queen Anne style. The impressively appointed public spaces are decked with chandeliers and antique furniture, and the interiors

A historic plaque at the Cornstalk Hotel.

are fashioned with salvaged fixtures from Louisiana sugar plantations. Canopy beds and stained-glass windows complete the look, and you, too, can look from the front of the house, with longing in your heart for the cornfields of Iowa.

Lagniappe

Employees report cold spots in a couple of the bedrooms, and there are stories of ghostly children that have been seen running through the building and the grounds. The most startling/unbelievable story reported on the haunted New Orleans websites, though, is that some guests have discovered that when they looked at the photos from the camera they had with them, among the photographs were pictures of themselves asleep in their beds. It is creepy that nineteenth-century children would know how to work digital cameras, but then, you know how naturally kids take to technology.

12.
THE BOURBON ORLEANS HOTEL

Bewitching brunettes with eyes that ravished even the anchorites, languishing blondes with tender grace, led the brave Creole boys through the mazy labyrinths of love.
Lafcadio Hearn, 1885

It's hard to believe, walking amid the lurid chaos of Bourbon Street today, that two hundred years ago, it was home to some of the classiest events in town. Sure, there's the odd oasis of sophistication if you catch things at the right time, though if you've ever actually been to the Friday lunch at high-end restaurant Galatoires, you'll know the rich people inside are just as sloppy drunk as the bovine masses outside. They're just drinking more expensive hooch.

The year is 1817, and the varied and voracious social scene that was already building up in the city was in need of venues in which to let its collective hair down. Some of the larger hotels were already catching on to the fact that hosting society balls instead of, say, cock fighting, was something of a money-spinner, as did local entrepreneur John Davis.

He had just opened his newest venture—the Orleans Ballroom. Even as it received its first revelers, it quickly became the backdrop to some of the most exclusive events in the city's calendar, which then, as now, was no mean feat. Its rota included, well, an embarrassment of balls. It hosted masquerade balls, carnival balls and the famous quadroon balls, where wealthy Creole gentlemen went through the arduous task of selecting mistresses from the assembled ranks of fair-skinned African-American women.

NEW ORLEANS HISTORIC HOTELS

The lobby of the Bourbon Orleans Hotel.

Within a decade, the venue was so respected and prestigious that it had been commandeered as a state and house legislative meeting place. As with so many events involving major historical figures in New Orleans, there is no official documentation, but it is said that Andrew Jackson announced his candidacy for president of the United States of America within these walls.

Flush with his undeniable successes, Davis started to expand his empire. The St. Louis was competing with him by staging its own elegant balls and diversification was required. He duly acquired the adjacent plot of land and built a new theater—namely, the Théâtre d'Orléans, the Orleans Theatre. He must have assumed his touch to be Midas-like, as triumph followed triumph—the sounds of elaborate French opera productions flooded out from the windows of his theater's great hall and its gaming rooms surpassed most of the local competition.

Lafcadio Hearn, being a notable man about town, was among the visitors on whom Mr. Davis and his enterprises left a lasting impression. As he notes in his *Historical Sketch Book and Guide to New Orleans* in 1855:

> In 1826 there was another place here that was equally as popular a place of resort, particularly of the jeunesse dorée, the young bloods of that day, and that was John Davis', on Orleans street, between Royal and Bourbon, where the Criminal Court once was. Mr. Davis was the proprietor of the

theatre and ball-room adjoining, and not to know John Davis was not to know the Crescent City.

Hearn obviously spent quite some time in the establishments, and he went into detail about the female clientele, who he was obviously observing purely for research and anecdotal purposes. He noticed that the proliferation and concentration of beauty wasn't always without its drawbacks, especially when passionate young men got, shall we say, riled up. From his same 1855 publication:

Bewitching brunettes with eyes that ravished even the anchorites, languishing blondes with tender grace, led the brave Creole boys through the mazy labyrinths of love and jealousy to the merry music of the cachucha and waltz. On ball nights Orleans Street was ablaze with the light from the Opera House windows, and by midnight the floor was crowded with dancers. This was naturally a far worse place for duels than Maspero's, and it is almost impossible to enumerate the "affairs" which dated their origin from the ball-room and cafe, and from the smiles given by some coquettish fair one.

Davis quickly became a well-respected and eminent impresario, and one of the major promoters of French theater and opera in the city. In its first five seasons, for example, the theater presented 140 operas, with 52 American premiers being accounted for in that number. John Davis retired from managing the venue in 1837 and was replaced by his son, Pierre. In 1842, the only real competitors in town (the St. Charles Theatre and the New American Theatre) both burned down, giving Théâtre d'Orléans *de facto* dominance of the scene.

According to the city directory of the time, the venue was also operating as a hotel, taking in the visitors who no doubt traveled from far and wide to see this testament to the good times that were undeniably rolling in the middle of the French Quarter. The ballroom could be joined to the theater to form one enormous space for balls and events, and it enjoyed high praise, the architect Henry Latrobe for example, deeming it one of the best venues in America.

The aforementioned good times were, as is almost always the way with these things, not going to last forever. If there's one thing that really puts a damper on bustling and carefree nightlife, it's a civil war. The social fabric of the city unraveled in spectacularly depressing style, and Davis's small corner

NEW ORLEANS HISTORIC HOTELS

The bar of the Bourbon Orleans Hotel.

of high culture lay in metaphorical ruins in the case of the ballroom and in literal physical ruins in the case of the theater, which burned down in 1866.

In 1881, the mood was a little more somber in this corner of the Vieux Carré. The theater and ballroom had been acquired by the Sisters of the Holy Family for use as a school and convent—no opera, no gaming, just the schooling of orphans and being married to Christ.

According to one story, a nun was showing a visitor around the convent and stopped at what was then the chapel. "This is the old Orleans Ballroom," she said. "They say it is the best dancing floor in the world. It is made of three thicknesses of cypress. That is the balcony where the ladies and gentlemen used to promenade. Down there, on the banquette, the beaux used to fight duels."

The nuns stayed there for some time—eighty-three years, to be exact, only moving out when they needed to expand, such were the apparent boom times in the nunnery business.

In 1963, work began to transform the building into a new hotel. The ballroom was to be incorporated and the façade worked into the design of the Bourbon Orleans Hotel. The immediate future may not have held such heights as it had attained in its heyday, but there would at least be slightly more celebration and rowdiness than had taken place the last eighty-three

NEW ORLEANS HISTORIC HOTELS

The swimming pool at the Bourbon Orleans Hotel.

years, not to imply that the Sisters of the Holy Family didn't enjoy themselves now and then.

The hotel now occupies one of the most central blocks in the French Quarter and is one of the livelier hotels, given its location right on Bourbon Street. The ballroom still welcomes events of course, albeit more weddings and corporate shindigs than quadroon balls. It's hard to envision opera or nuns as you walk around the lobby with your to-go cup, but the celebratory party atmosphere of that golden age are never really far away.

Lagniappe

The Sisters of the Holy Family Order was established by four women in 1842. The order is now the oldest female-led African American order in America. Its first convent was a small building on Bayou Street, but it eventually moved to the building that had once housed the Orleans Ballroom. The old ballroom became the order's chapel. It moved to New Orleans East, where it remains, still dedicated to the community it has always served.

The hotel is a hotbed of paranormal activity, and there are said to be as many as fifteen to twenty separate ghosts roaming the hotel. Many of these are children, which, as we all know, are the rowdiest kind of ghosts. There is an impressive range of spectral diversity, and the spirits who roam the halls and rooms of the Bourbon Orleans represent all the different eras of this building's history.

There is the story of the Confederate soldier, or the "Man" (great imagination with the naming, there), that dwells on both the sixth and seventh floors. The children and female apparitions found at the hotel are most likely from the era when the Sisters of the Holy Family operated the convent, girls' school, medical ward and orphanage. The famous Orleans Ballroom, home to the grandest social events of the nineteenth century, is also home to a lonely ghost dancer, which is seen twirling underneath the ballroom's crystal chandelier.

13.
LE RICHELIEU

A large number of guests had been invited and a brass band was in attendance.
—Daily Picayune, *1902*

A sense of hospitality is practically engrained on the strip of land (the 1200 block of Chartres Street) where this hotel now stands. In fact, we can look all the way back to the mid-eighteenth century and find that there were primitive lodging houses in operation that took in American, French and Spanish soldiers at the time. The holy landladies and managers of the property were the Ursuline nuns—or, to give them their full title, the Sisters of St. Ursula—fresh off the boat from France to offer aid and salvation to their American-bound compatriots.

The land had been graciously given to them by a land grant in 1754, issued by none other than his majesty King Louis XV of France, on the understanding that the nuns set up care facilities for sick French soldiers, and create a school that would receive the young ladies of the day. When the terms are set out like that, it perhaps seems a little less gracious, but nevertheless, that was the arrangement.

In 1763, King Louis sneakily handed over Louisiana to his cousin Charles III of Spain. This news took around two years to reach the local French population, so while reaction was not swift, it was bloody. Spain was forced to send reinforcements, and some three thousand soldiers arrived under the command of Count Alexander O'Reilly, a good, traditional Spanish name if ever there was one.

NEW ORLEANS HISTORIC HOTELS

An exterior shot of the Richelieu Hotel.

A side note: Alexander was actually what was known as a "Wild Goose," referring to men who left Ireland to fight for foreign Catholic armies, initially joining Spanish forces fighting in Italy against the Austrians. He became known as Alejandro and rapidly ascended the ranks of the Spanish army.

O'Reilly wasted no time in his enthusiastic quelling of the rebellion and had a leading French figure and attorney general of the colony, Nicolas Chauvin de la Freniere, arrested and executed along with four of his henchmen. The hotel contends this took place in what is now the parking lot, but in any case, O'Reilly stamped his authority on the situation and quashed the "October Rebellion," the first of its kind on U.S. soil.

By the early 1820s, the rebellion movement was mainly water under the bridge, and the Ursuline nuns moved to another location in 1824, deeding the land, in a move that shocked no one, to the Catholic bishops of New Orleans. In true ecumenical style, the bishops promptly divided the land up into packages and sold the lots off to private citizens.

The bulk of the lots were bought in 1828 by Mr. John McDonough. The main things to know about Mr. McDonough are that he was absurdly rich, was considered wildly eccentric and was thought by the free-living Creoles to be something of a miser, which—spoiler alert—is usually how people get rich in the first place.

His frugality is, in fact, famously celebrated in another painting in the lobby of the hotel. It was painted by a local artist by the name of Carl

Cramer and depicts Mr. McDonough being rowed across the Mississippi from Algiers by one of his slaves, just so that he could save on the intrusive overhead of the five-cent ferry ride.

McDonough died in 1850, using his eccentricity for good by leaving his full estate to the cities of New Orleans and Baltimore so that they could establish public school systems. Children and schools in New Orleans still celebrate his birthday for this very reason.

The buildings that would form the foundation of the modern-day hotel began to take shape in 1845. Amusingly, before this could happen, and in a typically left-field New Orleans fashion, the land had to play host to a traveling circus, as reported in the *Louisiana Courier* of February 15, 1845:

> *Howe & Mabie's Circus: The extensive equestrian company of these managers is to commence performing this evening on a vacant square of ground in Conde between Hospital and Barracks, and under a spacious double pavilion, which is fitted up in novel style and lit by gas. Olympic Arena and New York Circus, Howe and Maybie, managers...opening February 15, 1845.*

The circus having vacated the lot, Dominique Lanata built five identical houses in a row, facing Chartres Street. It is recorded that they were to house

The lobby of the Richelieu Hotel.

his family, meaning he either had a lot of close brothers and sisters or he was extremely busy doing his own work for the good of the human species.

The houses had some prestige attached to them, being as they were the very first Greek Revival buildings to be erected in the French Quarter. One of these original houses is now the lobby and bar area of the ground floor, and the Richelieu has three suites on its second floor.

In time, the lots next door were also developed, but with a more commercial enterprise in mind. A family by the name of Cusimano bought the land in 1902 and built a macaroni factory at the corner of Chartres and Barracks Streets. It wasn't just any macaroni factory, mind you; it was the largest macaroni factory that the United States had ever seen. In true New Orleans style, and given that no excuse for a party has ever been passed up, even a macaroni factory got a celebratory welcome, as the *Daily Picayune* of August 1902 noted:

> *Yesterday afternoon a new macaroni manufactory, the largest in the United States, was opened at the corner of Chartres and Barracks Streets...*[the] *three story brick building constructed for the purpose is the property of J. Cusimano. The building is 164 feet long by 64 feet in width and is equipped with the most modern and labor saving devices for the manufacture of macaroni. The first floor is devoted entirely to the manufacture of macaroni. The third floor is used for drying, and the second for packing, and about 30 men are employed.*
>
> *A large number of guests had been invited and a brass band was in attendance. The galleries surrounding the building were decorated with American and Italian flags and bunting and the banquet was spread on the second floor. The building as well as the machinery, etc. was erected under the supervision of Mr. Robert Palestine, an architect and engineer who received his training in Europe. Mr. Cusimano came to New Orleans as a small boy about 22 years ago.*

The Cusimanos had bought the land from the Duplessis family, who were, in a convenient turn of events, distant relatives of Cardinal Richelieu himself, a neat foreshadowing of our story's outcome. The factory turned out macaroni until 1939, having been rebuilt in 1909 after the destructive fire that French Quarter buildings have written into their histories as a matter of course. It became a furniture factory and then a mattress factory, but its days as a component of the American manufacturing industry were soon to come to an end.

NEW ORLEANS HISTORIC HOTELS

In 1963, the building became a hotel under the purchase and management of Mr. Sam Recile, who named it the Richelieu Apartment Hotel. The name is a tribute to the grandly named Armand-Jean du Plessis, Cardinal-Duke of Richelieu and prime minister to Louis XIII of France. Besides presumably having the eighteenth century's largest business cards, the cardinal is credited with being one of the influential architects of one of France's undeniable golden ages.

If you visit the hotel, you'll notice that the honorable gentleman is dignified even further by a striking portrait in the lobby of the hotel, inspired by a 1635 work by Philippe de Champaigne, which hangs in the Louvre in Paris.

Mr. Recile was a typically colorful New Orleans character, a euphemism on which we won't dwell too much here. Having moved to the city when he was fourteen, it is reported that he started buying property in his mother's name when he was sixteen and that he oversaw the drilling of his first oil well when he was just nineteen.

At this time, and in a flurry of activity that would shame most teenagers, he was also busy constructing a building on Harrison Avenue that eventually housed, among other commercial concerns, a record store that was owned by Mr. Harry Connick Sr.

Come 1963, he was doing sterling work with his new hotel on Chartres Street—so much so, in fact, that in 1965, the Vieux Carré Commission presented him with an "Honor Award for Renovation."

A room at Le Richelieu Hotel.

It didn't receive universal praise, however, as a stern letter to the *Times-Picayune* from February 5, 1964, shows. The author is listed as a Captain Earl W. Garvin: "As a former owner of the property at 1228 Chartres, we have heard with consternation about plans to build the Richelieu Hotel on land formerly occupied by a furniture factory at Barracks and Chartres."

Captain Garvin's objections were roundly ignored, and in 1969, Recile had himself a successful hotel to sell on to a couple of fellow New Orleanians, Frank Rochefort Jr. and Gerald Senner, who further renovated the hotel under the umbrella of the Richelieu Corporation.

It was around this time that a much larger-scale development was being touted. Reports from the *Times-Picayune* in February 1967 talked about the possibility of Le Richelieu Square, which would occupy the entire block bounded by Chartres, Barracks, Decatur and Governor Nichols Streets. The developers foresaw flagstone walkways taking guests between pools, gardens and patios, but this was a marketing strategy marketed more at luxury residential homes.

The eventual restoration and hotel opening was part of a larger trend in the 1960s in New Orleans, whereby several historic buildings in the Quarter became independent hotels, the larger chains kept at bay on Canal Street thanks to the strict laws surrounding renovation and construction.

That said, at eighty-six rooms, it is one of the larger French Quarter hotels and is still a striking building thanks in part to its deep-red exterior. The rooms have period furnishings, and the owners have lovingly maintained a sense of place and class.

Lagniappe

As well as the execution of La Freniere and his band of rebels, another story goes that a band of mutinous Spanish soldiers were also shot for, well, mutiny, on this site. Although ghostly sightings have not been reported in the hotel rooms themselves, supposedly some of the Spanish soldiers have been spotted walking around the bar area and, even more disconcertingly, around the swimming pool. This could just as likely be incredibly pale European tourists.

One of the original Greek Revival houses has a suite that was home to the musician Paul McCartney ("of Beatles fame" as the hotel helpfully points out) and his family for around two and a half months.

John McDonogh published a set of guidelines that he lived by, entitled *Rules for My Guidance in Life*, which was kind of like *The Habits of Successful People* for the early nineteenth century. Here they are:

> *Remember always that labor is one of the conditions of our existence. Time is gold; throw not one minute away, but place each one into account. Do unto all men as you would be done by. Never put off till tomorrow what you can do today. Never bid another do what you can do yourself.*
>
> *Never covet what is not your own. Never think any matter so trivial as not to deserve notice. Never give out that which does not first come in. Never spend but to produce. Let the greatest order regulate the transactions of your life. Study in your course of life to do the greatest possible amount of good. Deprive yourself of nothing necessary to your comfort, but live in honorable simplicity and frugality.*

14.
ANDREW JACKSON FRENCH QUARTER HOTEL

So another landmark in New Orleans is being demolished to make room for a modern building. It is the old United States Court building in which General Jackson was fined $1,000 for contempt of court.
—*Daily States, 1888*

It wouldn't be New Orleans without at least one hotel named after the general (and future president of the United States) who became a national hero when he defeated the British at the Battle of New Orleans. However, the hotel was thus named after being the site of a less honorable episode in Jackson's illustrious career.

The building, used as a boarding school in the late eighteenth century and now listed on the National Register of Historic Places, is in fact located on the site of a famous city courthouse, the very place where our leading man, Major General Andrew Jackson, was once indicted for contempt of court and charged with obstruction of justice.

The case occurred during the tenure of U.S. attorney John Dick. In 1815, just after the Battle of New Orleans, Dick indicted Jackson on charges of obstruction of justice and contempt of court. According to the indictment, Jackson had "disrespectfully wrested from the clerk an original order of the honorable judge of this court, for the issuing of a writ of *habeas corpus* in the case of a certain Louis Louallier, then imprisoned by the said Major General Andrew Jackson."

This was seemingly a clear case of contempt, and Jackson further incurred the charges of obstruction when he went all in and with a flagrant

A shot of the modern day exterior of the Andrew Jackson Hotel. *Paul Oswell.*

The sign of the Andrew Jackson Hotel. *Paul Oswell.*

disregard for authority, imprisoned the very judge who had charged him with contempt. Showing the steely reserve and determination that had made him so renowned, the future president of the United States appeared in court, refused to answer any questions and promptly received a fine of $1,000.

The courthouse stood until 1888, when it was sold and almost immediately torn down. Even in those days, there was some dismay that an apparently

NEW ORLEANS HISTORIC HOTELS

An exterior view of the Andrew Jackson Hotel. *Paul Oswell.*

historic building was being lost forever to some new carbuncle that would no doubt bring the tone of the neighborhood down.

An editorial in the *Daily States* from October 1888 says as much:

> *So another landmark in New Orleans is being demolished to make room for a modern building. It is the old United States Court building in which General Jackson was fined $1,000 for contempt of court. The building, in which this incident occurred is an old one-story building with a Spanish roof, was secured by the United States at the time of the cession made by France.*
>
> *On the 2nd of January 1829, the property was publicly sold to Chevalier Louis d'Aquin, the patent of the sale being signed by J.Q. Adams, President of the United States. After changing hands many times it finally became the property of Mr. Henry Pfeffer, who now demolishes the old building to erect a two story brick building to be used for a store and residence.*

Stores and residences hardly reflect the drama of a future president being fined for contempt of court, but such was progress. The *Daily States* was prescient, though, and the building had a fairly characterless life. Henry Pfeffer sold the place in 1954 for $22,000, and the latest recorded bill of sale dates to 1959, when the building was acquired by Arthur Steiner for $37,100. The hotel itself doesn't have records of when it opened in its present incarnation, but likely it was a short time after the 1959 sale, when historic hotel conversions in the Quarter were all the rage.

The building these days is a peer of similar conversions, such as the neighboring Cornstalk Hotel, and since the French Quarter ordinances forbid any modernization of exteriors, it's unlikely to draw any further complaints from local residents about local landmarks being torn down.

Lagniappe

Five children lost their lives in a devastating fire in the late 1700s when the building was a school. Hotel guests have reported hearing children playing in the courtyard in the middle of the night, and one said that he saw a ghostly child watching television. Ghosts these days, eh? They really need to get outside more.

15.
THE LAFITTE GUEST HOUSE

The building contract called for the building to be painted red, penciled and fitted with shutters painted Paris Green.
—*Vieux Carré Survey*

In 1848, architect Robert Seaton was commissioned by Paul Joseph Gleises and his wife, Marie Odalie Ducayet, to build them a home. Little expense was spared, and the budget was an impressive sum at almost $12,000. Yes, certainly many buildings in the area would have cost much more, but a single family putting down this much money on an exclusive residence would certainly have set tongues wagging.

The comments from the local gossips might not always have been of the kindest nature, either. Gleises had a job with the New Orleans Gas Company as a "collector of debts," which is probably not as sinister a profession as it sounds, but in any case it was in no way anything like the high-ranking vocation that would allow for such showboating.

The family money almost certainly came from his father, a first-generation French immigrant who just happened to be the most respected coach maker in the city. Yes, daddy's dealership worked out well for young Paul, who was able to impress and furnish his wife with a lavish town house after just a couple years of marriage.

Marie Ducayet, by the way, was from a very prominent and respected family who lived in a well-appointed plantation house in what is now Bayou St. John. At least, this was true when Gleises met her. The family subsequently fell on hard times, and Gleises—nothing if not an opportunist,

NEW ORLEANS HISTORIC HOTELS

An exterior shot of the Lafitte Guest House. *Paul Oswell.*

it would seem—ended up buying that house as well, though he generously allowed her family to remain there until he sold it.

Back to the residence that was to become the Lafitte Guest House, though—imagine the bragging rights some ten years later when Seaton paired up with James Gallier Jr. and completed work on the French Opera House on Bourbon and Toulouse Streets. This professional partnership thrived and went on to construct the famous Gallier House, the eclectic architecture of which can still be seen to this day on the 1100 block of Royal Street. The latter was originally the home of Gallier himself and is now a popular visitor's attraction and a National Historic Landmark.

For the Gleises building, Seaton used a builder called Peebles according to the Vieux Carré Digital Survey: "Joshua Peebles was the builder, according to the plans of architect R. Seaton, for this grand 3½-story Greek Revival townhouse with front and side galleries. The building contract called for the building to be painted red, penciled and fitted with shutters painted 'Paris green.'"

Having a house that had been designed and built by such a highly sought-after architect—one that was connected with the high arts no less—could not have hurt the resale value of the property, and no doubt Gleises dined out on this very desirable connection.

Nothing much of any note had stood on the land before Gleises bought it and ordered work on his home to begin. A humble family residence had

The sign of the Lafitte Guest House. *Paul Oswell.*

been there, one resident of note being Bernard Marigny, whose land-buying empire stretched out past Esplanade Avenue to form the neighborhood that became a fashionably expensive part of the city—the Fauborg Marigny.

Marigny or no Marigny, though, the nondescript house was quickly demolished and work began afresh in 1848, taking around a year to complete. Previous to the house that no one really cared for, the land had been the site of Charity Hospital (a gift from the kindly king of Spain in 1793), but given the obvious occupational hazard of being a building in those days, the property burned down in 1809.

Let's take a tour of the Gleises new house. The first floor holds their kitchen, along with the functional amenities of the day such as the stable (no doubt Paul could get a fairly decent discount on a new coach to store there) and a coal house. The second and third floors (yes, it was a grand three-story affair) were the residential quarters with living, dining and bedrooms. There was also an attached wing, which was also three stories tall but presumably far less sumptuous. This annex housed the family's slaves and, subsequently, servants.

NEW ORLEANS HISTORIC HOTELS

The Gleises were apparently very happy there and, in a show of commendable fertility, raised six children. A decade later as the Civil War brewed, the family moved to Philadelphia and then on to New York, and although they retained ownership of the house until they (the deeds had been passed on to Marie) sold it in 1866, they never did return to New Orleans. Just for the record, Paul lived to seventy-eight, dying in 1898, while Marie took longevity even further, living until she was ninety years old.

The house went through many owners and incarnations for the next hundred years, sadly none of them doing anything of note beside quietly living there, showing little regard for the work of future historians of the property. In the late 1960s, it came under the management of Andrew Crocchiolo and Edward Doré until the late '70s. They left the house for a twenty-year period to pursue other interests. After managing major hotels throughout the country, including the Waldorf Astoria in New York City and the historic Griswald Inn in Connecticut, they returned to Lafitte Guest House as hosts once more.

The guesthouse now lies on the outer rim of what is affectionately known as the "Fruit Loop," the collection of gay bars that help give Bourbon Street at least some variety beyond strip joints and, well, straight bars. It's at the unmarked checkpoint where Bourbon Street starts to quiet down and become—hard to believe if you don't live here—residential.

It is handily situated across from the oldest bar in New Orleans, and one of the few tolerable drinking spots on Bourbon Street if you dislike shots of

The lobby of the Lafitte Guest House. *Paul Oswell.*

primary-colored liquor and loud cover bands, Lafitte's Blacksmith Shop. The clamor of Bourbon thins out here, and you can actually imagine something of what life was like here in a time before karaoke machines.

The house draws its name from the bar, which draws its name from the rumor that the pirate Jean Lafitte once owned the building that the bar resides in, though as with most stories about pirates and outlaws, there's a distinct lack of written evidence to support this. Still, it makes a good story, and in the end, the romance of the times are hardly dictated by whether Lafitte actually owned the building or just drank and plotted there.

The artistic spirit of Robert Seaton, and I think we can safely presume he had one, lives on today in a beautiful lobby art gallery, filled as it is with the works of local and international artists. It's a tasteful slice of old New Orleans, and the tour guides' carriages still pass by today, a fitting testament to the occupation of Gleises senior, whose carriages paid for a substantial part of the original building.

Lagniappe

The property owners tell the legend of a mother and two of her children who all died in what is now Room 21, which should still be fine for most visitors as long as it doesn't get too much more upsetting. Oh wait, it actually does get way more upsetting. One of the children died in the yellow fever epidemic of 1853, and her sibling apparently hanged herself. Unsurprisingly, the mother of these unfortunates grieved for the remainder of her life, and it's said that she died of a broken heart some years later. The proprietors say that guests and employees report crying coming from the room, along with "an intense feeling of despair." So it's probably not the best recommendation for honeymooners.

It's also said that the girl who died of yellow fever appears in the mirror outside Room 21, and there are reports of lights operating on their own, switched on and off by the mother, who is still grieving for her daughters (and, presumably, is baffled by what light switches are).

16.
PLACE D'ARMES HOTEL

The little college which I have established at New Orleans well pleases everyone.
—*Father Raphael de Luxembourg, 1725*

In the heart of the French Quarter, Place D'Armes Hotel is located in what was also the heart of New Orleans in the 1700s and 1800s, and it was in fact the site of the first school in New Orleans, opening some time around 1725.

The building itself is a little older. In 1724, it had been the property of Augustin Langlois, a Canadian who came here while quite young with his two brothers. In 1725, Father Raphael de Luxembourg, rector of the St. Louis Parish Church, acquired the structure from Augustin Langlois, and it was here that his order, the Capuchin Fathers, established an early and important school.

Mr. Samuel Wilson, Jr., writing of this very site in *The Capuchin School in New Orleans, 1725* says:

> On a site now numbered 617–619 St. Ann Street, opposite the Presbytere, between Chartres and Royal Street[s], there once stood a small frame house erected by one of the first settlers in French Colonial New Orleans. It was probably like most of the houses of those first years, a simple building built with a heavy wood frame "sur sol" or on ground sills, timbers laid directly on the ground, the frame mortised and tennoned and pegged together, covered on the outside with wide boards, its steep roof covered with wood shingles or strips of bark.

NEW ORLEANS HISTORIC HOTELS

An exterior shot of the Place D'Armes Hotel. *Paul Oswell.*

This is the earliest reference to a school in New Orleans after the founding of the city in 1718, and the laying out of its streets in 1721 seems to be contained in the lengthy letter that Father Raphael, who was the superior of the Capuchin missions in Louisiana, addressed from New Orleans on September 15, 1725, to the Abbé Raguet, ecclesiastical director of the Company of the Indies.

Father Raphael wrote:

> *I have just made an establishment for a little school at New Orleans. To direct it I have found a man who knows Latin, mathematics, drawing [and] singing and whose handwriting is fairly good...I have proposed to him that he should devote himself to the education of youth in our mission...he accepted this offer joyfully, and in the two or three months that he has been with us I have been able to do nothing but congratulate myself on his application to his duties.*

In another letter to the Abbé Raguet, Father Raphael wrote:

> *The little college which I have established at New Orleans well pleases everyone. Exercises are done there with much order and these young people are already giving great hopes. But I do not know where to find wherewith to reimburse the sum which I have been obliged to impress in*

NEW ORLEANS HISTORIC HOTELS

The gardens at the Place D'Armes Hotel. *Paul Oswell.*

order to buy the house which serves for class and seminary. It has cost three thousand livres. I have paid eight hundred of it in bills which have been given to us before.

By 1740, the schoolhouse and the fence surrounding it had fallen into ruin, and by 1753, the churchwardens were selling the property. It may have been purchased at that time by Jean Baptiste Destrehan, treasurer of the Royal Navy. At any rate, by 1765 his son, Jean Baptiste Honore Destrehan, inherited what was a spacious estate with an impressive French colonial dwelling of brick and colombage, a coach house, and a kitchen, undoubtedly surrounded by gardens and all the outbuildings belonging to such an establishment.

In 1776, after the death of the Destrehan son, this corner was sold to Pedro de Marigny, who went to work erecting a more sophisticated property, though in 1788, the whole corner was burned down in the Good Friday fire, and what had become an elaborate collection of cottages and courtyards was destroyed.

The redeveloped land passed through the hands of Julien Poydras, the noted Louisiana philanthropist, though when he owned it, it wasn't, according to the *Vieux Carré Digital Survey*, much more than "a brick house of two stories and a two story brick kitchen in the yard."

Julien Poydras died a few months after buying the place, and the entire plot was partitioned into smaller portions. These are the buildings seen on

NEW ORLEANS HISTORIC HOTELS

The courtyard fountain at the Place D'Armes Hotel. *Paul Oswell.*

maps dating around 1876, buildings which must have been further destroyed after 1908, only to be replaced by a wine storage warehouse.

The warehouse seemingly stood there for almost sixty years and really wasn't a building of any note, the next major development being in 1963, when plans were announced for a five-story motel. Originally called the Jackson Square Motoro Hotel, it opened in 1964 as the Place D'Armes Motor Hotel, eventually becoming, simply, the Place D'Armes. Its most notable feature is its beautiful courtyard, one of the most lush in the French Quarter and worth dipping into for some tranquility whenever you're passing.

Lagniappe

Place D'Armes was the original name of what is now Jackson Square. It was here that important parades and ceremonies (usually of a military nature) were held. The square had its original name until 1851, when it was renamed for Andrew Jackson and his statue was erected there. The square is now a National Historic Landmark.

17.
FURTHER HISTORIC HOTELS

SHORT STORIES

THE DAUPHINE ORLEANS

Records of the Dauphine Orleans's site date back to 1775, the initial owners being among the first families of the city's Spanish and French settlements, and some of the original structures still stand today in the form of the cottages. In the early nineteenth century, these were apparently used as boarding- and guesthouses. An early resident was the naturist and bird hunter John James Audubon, who painted his famous *Birds of America* series there from 1821 to 1822.

He was a poor artist in those days, living in rented rooms, and remember that all that ammunition for shotguns didn't come cheap (dead birds make much better models than live ones, after all). The cottage is now known as the Audubon Room and serves as the hotel's breakfast room, though the menu is distinctly light on poultry and game.

The fourteen Hermann House Guest Rooms, located across the street from the hotel's main building, were originally built in 1834 to serve as the town home of a prosperous merchant, Samuel Hermann. The original building contract outlines Mr. Hermann's very detailed instructions, including a near-pathological interest in the size of the nails and the number of coats of paint he required. He also demanded that only the "best country brick, sand and cypress" be used in the building's construction.

The hotel was situated in the middle of Storyville and although records show it was a private residence for much of this time, it's safe to say that it probably saw its share of wanton goings-on in and around its walls. The end of this period marked an upcoming half decade of inactivity for the neighborhood and the property, and it wasn't until some sixty years later that anything of note happened.

In August 1969, the *States Item* announced that "balconied French Quarter townhouses will form part of the façade of the new Dauphine Orleans Motor Hotel at 415 Dauphine which opens formally today. The new luxury motel facility has 94 guest rooms and suites; a dining room and lounge; swimming pool and on-site parking for 100 cars."

The hotel became formally known as the Dauphine Orleans in February 1971. At the time of writing, it was part of the prestigious New Orleans Hotel Collection, along with the Audubon Cottages, which form a kind of exclusive annex to this solid French Quarter property.

Lagniappe

There's quite the variety of spirits apparently wandering about the hotel. Guests have reported seeing everything from Civil War soldiers to—unsurprising, given its Storyville location—spectral ladies of the night.

One regular haunt is that of a Creole soldier who wanders through the courtyard wearing a military uniform. Another spirit is a female, who goes one better than wandering and dances across the courtyard.

The hotel reports that: "Parapsychologist Dr. Larry Montz, founder of the International Society For Paranormal Research, conducted an investigation at the Dauphine Orleans Hotel and reported several spirits, among them a soldier, general or other high ranking officer, wearing a dark uniform that could have been from the War of 1812 or Civil War. His name might be Eldridge. He walked with the investigative team by the pool area and back through to the cottages."

THE COLUMNS

If you're heading uptown on the rattling streetcar, there's a striking building that you'll pass at 3811 St. Charles Avenue. On the terrace, there's likely all manner of well-heeled people and perhaps the odd scruffy travel writer enjoying a drink, set as it is a tasteful ways back from the road and tracks.

There's a streetcar stop right there, so if you have no alternative plans, I strongly suggest you get off the streetcar here and join them.

This is the illustrious Columns Hotel, once the dream house of a local tobacco merchant, Simon Hernsheim. He spared little in the way of expense when constructing this impressive abode, which was completed in 1883. For fifteen years it was a lively home where Hernsheim entertained friends and guests with relish, and with a house like this one, it's little wonder you'd want to show it off.

The Hernsheim family sold the place in 1898, and after a series of residential owners, in the early twentieth century it became an upscale boardinghouse, a world away from the cramped conditions and downtown shenanigans of the French Quarter. Granted, many people like being around downtown shenanigans, but for the more urbane traveler to New Orleans, this was a haven of gentility and refinement.

Over the years, it slowly transitioned into a full-service hotel, and though it fell into some disrepair, it was bought and fully restored by the current owners, Claire and Jacques Creppel, in 1980. You can only sell charming faded elegance for so long before it just becomes unwelcoming dilapidation, after all. If you can't stay, an afternoon or early evening cocktail on that elegant porch is still highly recommended.

Lagniappe

As befits such a genteel property, even the ghosts here are described as having "impeccable Southern manners." Apparently a well-dressed gentleman politely checks up on guests, a lady in white reminisces about her life there in one of the lounges and a small girl walks about on the balcony. You just can't beat Uptown spirits for being the best spectral hosts.

Bienville House

Beginnings don't come too much more humble than being a building used to store grain, but this former warehouse was nothing more grand than just that when it was built in the early nineteenth century. The storage facility was originally owned by Planters Rice Mills, the space subsequently becoming home to Thompson's Rice Mill and Southern Syrup Manufacturing—so far, so boringly commercial.

NEW ORLEANS HISTORIC HOTELS

An exterior shot of the modern-day Bienville House.

In modern times, a boutique hotel opening in a former grain warehouse would be the height of hipster development and make the travel pages of many a style magazine, but in 1835, when the building was transformed into the North American Hotel, it was a much more prosaic occasion.

A notice in the *New Orleans Bee* announces the arrival of the hotel under the auspices of a small group of French entrepreneurs, who were transferring their business from another location: "REMOVAL. The subscriber has removed from No. 30 Toulouse Street to his new Hotel, corner of Bienville and the Levee, which will soon be ready for the reception of Boarders and Lodgers."

The hotel immediately began advertising, making the most of its riverside location and with one eye on the warmer months ahead, one newspaper display in the *Louisiana Courier* called it "a delightful summer residence for Ladies and Gentlemen. Situated at the corner of Bienville Street, in the center of business and commanding a full view of all shipping and steamboats in the river."

In fact, this was just the beginning of a tidal wave of praise with which the *Louisiana Courier* from April 1837 went on to swamp the North American Hotel:

NEW ORLEANS HISTORIC HOTELS

The swimming pool at the Bienville House.

> *The hotel combines the greatest advantages for salubrity and convenience, and the interior arrangements are of such a nature that they cannot fail to give complete satisfaction…The subscriber is determined to persist, with indefatigable exertions, to render the North American Hotel perfect in every respect, so that it cannot be surpassed by any similar establishment in the United States."*

By 1837, the owners were ready to move on, and interested parties were invited to make an offer to one of the owners, who came complete with the regulation, nineteenth century hotel–owning first name: Jean Baptiste Étienne Germain Musson. From the December 7, 1837 *New Orleans Bee*:

> *For Rent. The whole of that large and spacious house, or, if preferred, that portion fronting the river, situated at the corner of Bienville and Public Road, well known as the North American Hotel, the premises are undergoing suitable repairs and will now be ready in a few days. For terms apply to G. Musson, 89 Customhouse Street.*

133

NEW ORLEANS HISTORIC HOTELS

The lobby of the Bienville House.

The building was split into a small French Quarter hotel (called the Desoto, not to be confused with the hotel of the same name that became Le Pavillon) for boarders and a firehouse. As far as we can tell from records, this hotel was still operating in 1881, and probably did so until its sale in 1902.

Eventually the building would become the Royal Bienville, twenty luxury apartments that marked the revival of Decatur Street. By the early 1970s, the building was once again a New Orleans hotel that appealed to people driving to or through the city. After surviving a fire that destroyed a warehouse across the street, the eighty-two-room "motor hotel" was purchased by the Monteleone family in 1972.

The new owner was William A. Monteleone, who established his wunderkind twenty-year-old son, William A. Monteleone Jr., as the fourth generation of the Monteleone family to run hotels.

William Jr. had started in the hotel business at age fourteen while attending school. In a quote from the November 1972 *Times-Picayune*, he laid out his perfectly reasonable expectations for the venture saying, "All my life, I've had one ambition: to have the best hotel in the world."

The Bienville House hotel is still family-owned and operated by the Monteleone family.

Lagniappe

One paranormal investigator reports having been stared at in his sleep by a ghostly presence, and there are the regulation-issue spirits walking through walls.

In terms of ghostly goings-on, Room 356 is reportedly the "most active" of several of the eighty-three rooms.

HOTEL PROVINCIAL

Originally acquired by the seemingly omnipresent Ursuline nuns, a building was constructed to serve as a military hospital around 1722. There is anecdotal evidence to suggest that a short time later, it had been turned into a coffee merchant's warehouse and store. This would seemingly coincide with the bill of sale to the Company of the West Indies, which relates to a 1731 transfer of the title.

A shot of the exterior of the modern-day Hotel Provincial. *Paul Oswell.*

NEW ORLEANS HISTORIC HOTELS

A change of ownership between non-scandalous owners aside, the trail goes fairly cold until an advertisement in the *Louisiana Courier* from December 11, 1816, which reveals a surprising and dramatic change of business practices:

> *NOTICE. FELIX, Ladies Hair dresser. Ladies wishing to have their hair dressed at his house, will please apply to his wife to appoint the hour. The price is two dollars. He also informs that he cuts gentlemen's hair for a dollar at their houses, and 50¢ at his shop…he lives in Mme. Carrick's house* [on] *Conde Street opposite Mr. Moreau's.*

We can only assume a fairly successful run for Mr. Felix and his colleagues, with no news of a change of commerce for quite some time. The lot burned down in 1874, though records show that a good barber's shop was not to be put down so easily and that it was trading again in the same spot in 1875.

Whether or not hair was still being cut there in 1902 is unclear, but what isn't in doubt is that the building was then purchased by the French Market Ice Manufacturing Company of New Orleans.

Even given the epidemic of fires that took place in the French Quarter on a seemingly weekly basis, you'd think an icehouse would be fairly resistant to the threat of burning down. You'd be wrong, as this cutting from the *Times-Picayune* from November 6, 1927, shows:

> *Fire. 6:30, November 5. French Market Ice Manufacturing Company, 1024 Chartres Street. Damage chiefly to the building and equipment was estimated at $200,000. The fire started in the 3rd floor of the building which is about 30 feet in the rear of the street facing a courtyard, explosions of crude oil storage tank and an ammonia tank…the only two modern buildings in the square are the French Market Branch of the Whitney Bank and the La Stella Manufacturing Company, corner of St. Philip and Chartres.*

The rebuilt facility was used as storage for seed for some time before being sold to the Dupepe family in 1961. They opened the Provincial Motor Hotel that same year with the assistance of architect Donald Zimmer.

A 1961 report from the *New Orleans States Item* describes the opening, with a nod to the "let's make the new look old" trend that this 1960s generation of hotels all went with:

The courtyard of the Hotel Provincial. *Paul Oswell.*

> *The new structure doesn't "fight with" the old Ursuline Convent, it even has the same kind of dormer windows...they spared no time, effort, care nor [sic] expense on the details of the motel—its brickwork, paneling, railings and shutters are A No-1 in style and quality. There are enough arches and fan windows to please any visitor looking for "authentic" architecture of the 18th century, built in the 20th century.*

The modern-day hotel again pays tribute to its past with the name of its bar, the Ice House, and the building is now listed on the National Register of Historic Places. The current property has a grand lobby area and is particularly noted for its tropical courtyard.

Lagniappe

Hotel staff report that Building No. 5 is the most haunted. Anecdotal reports say that "many a guest say they have walked into their room and seen many bloody soldiers lying in pain and moaning in their room." If that doesn't warrant a call to housekeeping, I'm not sure what does.

HOTEL ST. PIERRE

In 1722, this Burgundy Street lot belonged to a sailor, Louis Roy, and the double masonry Creole cottage that had been constructed by 1830 has a regular succession of owners, none of whom appear to have lived dramatic lives or to have done anything noteworthy enough to make the local news. I'm not implying they weren't interesting people; I'm just saying that if they were, they were very discreet about what it was they were doing.

We can see that before it became the Hotel St. Pierre, the property was operating as the Crossbeam Motel (in 1969) and the Downtowner (1974). The owners of the former property were confident enough to open up the building for local inspection and general nosiness with this invitation in the *Times-Picayune* from November 17, 1969: "Crossbeam Motel Opens in Quarter: You are cordially invited to open the iron grill gates and step back into history at the Crossbeam Motel."

Probably the most interesting part of the building's past, though, is the fact that the back buildings housed the country's first jazz museum, which operated there from 1961 into the 1980s. Yet more cordiality is extended via a notice in the *Times-Picayune* from November 12, 1961: "You are cordially invited to attend ceremonies marking the opening of the New Orleans Jazz Museum, Sunday, November 12, 1961 [at] 2:30 p.m. at Congo (Beauregard)

An exterior shot of the St. Pierre Hotel. *Paul Oswell.*

A plaque commemorating the Jazz museum at the St. Pierre Hotel. *Paul Oswell.*

This plaque commemorates Louis Armstrong's visit to the St. Pierre Hotel. *Paul Oswell.*

Square, New Orleans, Louisiana…and on Sunday afternoon, the New Orleans Jazz Museum will be dedicated."

It was, in true New Orleans style, quite the occasion, as local *Times-Picayune* journalist Stella Martin reported on November 13, 1961: "Parade Opens Music Center: Museum Dedicated to History of Jazz: To the accompaniment of a rollicking rendition of 'Didn't He Ramble,' the clapping of many hands and a few jingles from the ankles of Sweet Emma the Bell Gal, the New Orleans Jazz Museum at 1017 Dumaine was formally dedicated and opened to the public."

For a city so proud of its jazz heritage, situating and maintaining a museum dedicated to jazz has proved a complicated and often frustrating process. In 1969, the museum relocated to the Royal Sonesta Hotel and then to an address on Conti Street, but that enterprise quickly went bankrupt.

The legacy of the 1961 site, though, lives on in the lobby of the St. Pierre Hotel, and if you wander in, you can still see plaques and several instruments that belonged to seminal jazz musicians, including a cornet owned by New Orleans's favorite son, Louis Armstrong. As with all jazz collections, it's more about the exhibits they *don't* show.

Lagniappe

Two resident spirits have been reported: one a Civil War Confederate soldier that inhabits the former slave quarters and the other just described as "a middle aged man" that apparently makes up for his anonymity by moving objects and changing the TV channel.

The Louisiana State Museum officially took over much of the collection of jazz artifacts in the 1980s, and much of it is housed in the museum's Jazz Collection, some of it on display in the Mint.

St. James Hotel

Built with the express intention of luring in local merchants and trades people, the hotel was originally built by New Orleans architect Charles Zimpel for Thomas Banks in 1833.

The Magazine Street side of the building was large enough to accommodate a number of stores and a glass-walled pedestrian arcade extended through the block. It was an environment conducive for business, with an on-site restaurant and a coffee room that apparently boasted the ability to accommodate up to five hundred people at one time. Thankfully, in those days before chai lattes and hazelnut mochas, coffee only came in a single form, so lines were kept to a minimum.

In 1843, the arcade was sold to Joseph Danforth Weaver and then to a coffee importation firm. Coffee was then, as now, a highly lucrative business, and this particular company was a major player in the industry, distributing beans to hundreds of local coffee shops around the country and undertaking the time-consuming and fraught negotiations that came with dealing with the coffee-producing countries.

In 1859, the Banks Arcade was renovated and the original St. James Hotel was built. The July 1860 *Times-Picayune* reported its opening:

> *The St. James Hotel raised its broad, imposing, handsome white stucco, five-story front, adorned on [the] first and second stories by large iron verandahs, 120 feet long. There were a barbershop, and in the rear, a fine bathing establishment. There were more than 250 gas-lit rooms and the double row facing on Magazine and on Arcade received through numerous windows a flood of light and air.*

It was undoubtedly a fine hotel, but any grandeur it may have had was short-lived. The Civil War in 1861 brought with it the attendant hardships, and until 1865, the hotel was used as a Union hospital. This development was reported by an intriguingly named 1867 publication, *Beauty and Booty*: "We have heard that the St. James Hotel and the Carrollton Hotel are to be converted into hospitals for their [Federals'] Sick soldiers. The new and costly furniture of the St. James is now being moved to Montgomery's Auction Mart for public sale."

The hotel was subsequently renamed the Vonderbank Hotel around 1883 (the *Daily States* called it a "small but elegant first class hotel"), and by 1894, the hotel had been renamed the Hotel Schmitt, after its new proprietor, John Schmitt. At some point the hotel changed hands again and reverted to its original name, the one by which it is known today.

To this day, the hotel retains a vaguely colonial aesthetic and some interior touches pay homage to the glory days (at least, this is how the British might refer to them) of the British West Indies.

Lagniappe

The hotel has its own legend. According to the story, a merchant named Che arrived in New Orleans during the influx of immigrants from the Caribbean during the nineteenth century.

Che had a shop on Magazine Street in the Banks Arcade and was infamous for his connections within the network of French merchants, infamous as he reputedly used insider knowledge to play them off one another and manipulate them.

One night in 1851, some disgruntled merchants set fire to Che's store, and when the smoke cleared, Che was nowhere to be seen. The news of the death of a Caribbean son led the highest local voodoo priestesses to conduct rituals to ensure that his spirit was carried home to the Caribbean, but for reasons that are never made clear, their procedure was interrupted.

From 1861 to 1865, during the Civil War, the hotel was used as a Union hospital. The story goes that in their last moments, soldiers would describe tropical visions of island heavens so beautiful that they entered into death quite willingly, seduced by the ethereal palm trees and crystal waters. It is believed that whatever portal the voodoo priestesses had opened for Che's spirit remained open and became a tunnel through which spirits of soldiers traveled into the next life, which promised sun, sand and surf.

Royal Sonesta

It won't come as anything of a shock to find out that New Orleans has a past fermented in alcohol. By the mid-1880s, the city—thanks to its influx of German immigrants—was the brewing capital of the South, and by 1890, there were about thirty breweries operating within the city limits.

One of them—Regal Brewing, owned by the American Brewing Company—once stood where the modern-day hotel stands now. Looking further back, the building had once been the site of a bakery, which was still a going concern as late as 1870, according to the *Daily Picayune* of the day:

> *That splendid and substantial one story brick property covered with slates situate*[d] *in Bourbon between Bienville, Conti and Royal streets Nos. 58 and 60 especially established as a bakery, presently occupied by Langles & Co. and containing in the main building 6 rooms, large carriage entrance*

on [the] *side, large brick stables with accommodations for at least a dozen horses, large two-story brick storerooms, 4 large ovens, kneading room, etc. privy, large paved yard, water works, etc. all in good working order.*

In fact the bakery business went back much further, as evidenced by this June 1841 clipping from the *Louisiana Courier*, calling the baked goods shop there "one of the oldest in the city":

BAKERY FOR SALE BY AUCTION BY S. GUINAULT. The stock in trade and establishment of the BAKE-HOUSE No. 73 Bourbon Street between Conti and Bienville streets. The concern is one of the oldest in New Orleans, in a central location, with a very good run of custom. A machine in making biscuits is attached. There are nine horses in good condition, and seven carts hung on springs, included in the establishment; besides a Dray and a Cart for hauling wood etc. Moreover, all the utensils, usually found in bake houses.

We know that there was an Orleans Coffee House next to the bakery (records show this in 1824, at least), and a wine and vinegar factory on the same block (owned by the appropriately named Mr. Charles Cavaroc) is present in 1883.

In any case, it's apparent that this was something of a gourmet corner, and any place that you could buy coffee, wine and bread all in one place was always going to be a popular spot.

In 1890, the American Brewing Company, makers of the very popular Regal Beer, purchased Mr. Cavaroc's winery. Through time, the brewery expanded into the neighboring historic yet deteriorating buildings, and it ultimately encompassed the entire frontages of Bienville, Bourbon and Conti Streets.

The brewery operated for decades before a decline through the 1950s and eventual closure in the 1960s. Little remained of the place in the late 1960s when Lester Kabacoff (who developed the Omni Royal Orleans) showed the property to the Sonnabends, part of the Sonesta family.

In 1967, the Vieux Carré Commission approved plans to develop a large hotel, and construction began on the $16 million Royal Sonesta Hotel. The exterior concept was a look reminiscent of typical 1830s New Orleans row houses. The Royal Sonesta Hotel New Orleans opened in September 1969.

Local jazz legend "Sweet Emma" Barrett cut the ribbon at the grand opening, which was part of a four-day celebration, culminating in a fundraising benefit for the Cultural Attractions Fund of New Orleans. As the *Times-Picayune*, reported, "They were all there—the Mayor, the councilmen, the politicians, the artists, the patrons of the arts, the old names and new of New Orleans society."

The modern-day hotel hosts a jazz legend of its own, housing the Irvine Mayfield Jazz Playhouse. The historic legacy of being a gourmet corner is also indirectly honored at one of the city's most prestigious restaurants, R'evolution.

Lagniappe

Only four men have served as the hotel's general manager. The first GM, James A. Nassikas, opened the property, followed by Earl Duffy (who served almost two years), Archie Casbarian (eight years) and now Hans Wandfluh.

The spot where the sales and catering office now resides (seventeen feet *below* sea level) was originally the home of the famous nightspot Economy Hall, where jazz greats such as Fats Domino used to perform. It also housed the New Orleans Jazz Museum, which continues to grow and can be found today in the Louisiana State Museum at the U.S. Mint.

The hotel is the birthplace of both the French Quarter Festival and the New Orleans Tourism and Marketing Corporation (NOTMC.)

PRINCE CONTI HOTEL

Since not all early nineteenth-century homes had private bathing facilities, public baths were an early feature of the French Quarter, and one of the most popular stood on the spot where the Prince Conti Hotel now stands. It appears that some existed previously to the notice that appeared in the *Daily Crescent*, announcing the opening of a new facility in 1849:

> *BATHS. The Public is respectfully informed that the splendid Baths recently erected in Exchange Alley, [on the] corner of Bienville Street, are now in operation. The proprietors of the Exchange Alley Baths are now erecting Bath Rooms on Conti Street near the corner of Dauphine, on the site formerly known as the Nepouilly* [Depouilly] *Baths, which, when completed, will excel in magnificence any establishment of the kind in the city.*

The building seems to have been a bathhouse for some time, in 1864 being called the Conti Street Hot Baths. In 1919, the facility was bought by the Grunewald Hotel and turned into a bathhouse for clothes, or what the majority of the English-speaking world might more sensibly refer to as a laundry. It's logical to assume that it was dedicated to cleaning the sheets and tablecloths of the Grunewald Hotel rather than being run as a commercial concern.

At around the same time, the Grunewald company also bought neighboring buildings that the official listings describe as a warehouse for its piano business.

The Prince Conti began its current incarnation at the same time as many of its small hotel peers in the Quarter. The early 1960s saw a swathe of these new motor hotels converted from older town houses—see also the Andrew Jackson, the Cornstalk Hotel, etc. A slang-heavy announcement of the opening somehow got into print in the shockingly casual *New Orleans States and Item*:

> *Prince Conti Motor Hotel Opens: People are still ga-ga over its 18th century lobby with* [its] *portrait of Prince Conti, painted in 1760, the Baccarat chandelier, armchairs upholstered in Aubusson tapestry* [and] *Louis XV mantel. Free parking within the building in real snorky* [see lagniappe] *surroundings is featured. You drive between Greek columns, potted plants, striped awnings and a fanciful bar known as the Prince's Bar.*

At some point, as with the other motor hotels in the city, the "motor" reference was dropped, and it operates today as a regular hotel.

Lagniappe

The present, seventy-six-room hotel includes the Bombay Club, a plush, colonial-themed martini bar.

I had to look up *snorky*, assuming it to be some hip slang of the day. It appears to mean "high class" and was a nickname that the gangster Al Capone gave to himself, possibly before syphilis rendered him less urbane.

18.
FRENCH QUARTER GUEST HOUSES

LAMOTHE HOUSE, INN ON URSULINES, INN ON ST. PETER, INN ON ST. ANN

There are four properties included in this charmingly idiosyncratic collection (all under one umbrella company), and the original buildings all date back to the early nineteenth century. They are as follows, with the dates we have for the original construction of the buildings that they are now housed in: the Lamothe House Hotel (constructed circa 1833), the Inn on Ursulines (circa 1816), the Inn on St. Peter (circa 1805) and the Inn on St. Ann (circa 1830).

The first recorded owner of the property that is now the Lamothe House, which stands at 621 Esplanade Avenue on the French Quarter/Marigny border, is Miss Marie Virginia Lamothe. She bought the land in 1829, selling it to her brother Jean, who, with his wealth amassed from his sugar cane plantation, had double town houses constructed on the site. A makeshift residence was built in 1833, with a much grander building going up in 1839.

Jean lived there, no doubt escaping the rigors of plantation life, for twenty years, eventually selling the property to a pair of Frenchmen, Paul Rivera and Henry Parlange, in 1859. This proactive pair went to town on the place, changing all the doors and shutters and converting the carriage entrance into the main entrance and hallway that you see today, which in its day was an incredibly radical move.

They didn't stop there, adding the standout Corinthian columns, the glorious twin winding stairways and the double entrance, which hides a multitude of period features that you'll find in few hotels around the city. The ceiling timbers, iron fastenings for windows and doors, rolled glass windowpanes and the great cypress

NEW ORLEANS HISTORIC HOTELS

Right: An exterior shot of the Lamothe House.

Below: An exterior shot of the Inn on Ursulines.

floors are all original fittings, well maintained and incredibly atmospheric. If you're staying, it's worth checking into the Antique Suite—if you can—which evokes the original elegance of those early town houses in keeping with the public spaces.

With some parts of the building being constructed in the late 1700s, the Inn on Ursulines is one of the oldest structures in the French Quarter. The Vieux Carré Digital Survey reveals the house that was there in 1816 was "composed of six rooms and a gallery, built in brick, between posts, and all other buildings to be found on this land."

Although it has gone through a long succession of residential and private owners, it remains a wonderful example of a very old, traditional Creole cottage. While it is the smallest of the French Quarter Guest Houses (it only has fifteen

An exterior shot of the Inn on St. Anne.

rooms), the Inn on Ursulines has been carefully restored and successfully displays the charm that it must have had. It has operated as a guest house since around 1990.

The Inn on St. Peter is listed on the National Register of Historic Places and was originally constructed in 1805 with its design influenced by the Spanish style of architecture during that period. The twenty-nine guestrooms here are arranged around the standout courtyards, and again, the property has mainly passed through private ownership.

The Inn on St. Anne is an 1840s, two-story side-hall town house, which was constructed by Étienne Courcelle for one Bernard de Santos. It has sixteen rooms and operated as a guesthouse in the 1980s under the name A Creole House. In addition to its guestrooms in the main property—some of which have original period touches, such as stone fireplaces—the hotel also owns a kind of annex, the Marie Leveau Apartments. The highlight of this hotel, though, is the Armstrong Suite, which boasts floor-to-ceiling windows opening onto a private balcony.

19.
THE JUNG AND THE RISE OF THE CANAL STREET HOTELS

Even as early as the 1830s, hotels were appearing on Canal Street, most of them near the river, including the Union Hotel and the Planters Hotel, which were located on Canal between Magazine and Tchoupitoulas.

Although most of the grander, more popular nineteenth-century properties were in the French Quarter, a few standout hotels, such as the Perry House, were on Canal. Canal, though, was there to cater to the needs of shoppers rather than incoming tourists needing somewhere to stay.

From Canal, you could just see the looming upper floors of the bigger hotels, which were set tastefully back from the main drag—the Grunewald (which became the Roosevelt) and the Monteleone, for example.

By the 1920s, there was a noticeable growth in the number of hotels on Canal. These included the LaSalle Hotel, the Hotel New Orleans and the Jung Hotel. By 1927, impressive cultural and entertainment centers had arrived, most notably in the shape of the famous Saenger Theatre, built for the phenomenal amount of $2.5 million and which re-created a fifteenth-century Italian courtyard and gardens. (The theater closed in 2005 after Hurricane Katrina but was fully restored and reopened in 2013.)

The LaSalle occupied the land next to the Saenger Theatre, and in fact, part of the theater was incorporated into the hotel building. It enjoyed business directly from the nearby Southern Railway terminal on Basin Street. The Hotel New Orleans (named the Marbeck for a time in the 1930s) later became the Amerihost Inn and Suites and, for a time in the 1990s, served as a dorm for Tulane University.

A postcard of the Jung Hotel, "The South's Largest and Finest Hotel," 1940s. *Postcard published by Albert Advertising Agency, Galveston, Texas.*

It was the Jung Hotel, though, that was the most prestigious Canal Street property in the 1920s. The hotel first opened its doors in 1907 and was built for Peter Jung Sr. and his family. Such was its popularity that 1925 saw the addition of an annex (followed by yet another in the 1960s). Ask people what they remember about the Jung Hotel, and they will almost all reply that they recall the elegant balls and dances that were held on its outstanding rooftop garden.

In the time before the large hotel chains moved in, it was the largest convention hotel in the South and was called the Jung for more than seventy-five years. Its subsequent incarnations were the Clarion, the Radisson and the Park Plaza. In common with the Roosevelt (in 2005 called the Fairmont), the Jung was heavily damaged in the levee failures of 2005, but unlike the Roosevelt, it never reopened.

The convention industry, spurred by the 1984 Louisiana World Exposition (World's Fair), continued to grow, mirroring the tourism industry and together creating the market for most of the larger chain hotels we see along Canal today.

20.
HOTELS IN MODERN-DAY NEW ORLEANS

As tourism continued to grow in the postwar era, New Orleans realized it had to act to prevent the "Disney-fication" of the French Quarter. As the local convention industry also began to grow in the 1960s, larger properties, such as the Governor House Motor Hotel and the International Hotel, were built. By the mid- to late 1960s, though, there was severe danger of the French Quarter's being lost to new development, and in an extreme move in 1969, the city decided to impose a moratorium on new hotels being built in the historic neighborhood.

Although lip service was certainly paid to the idea of preservation, every so often, the sheer financial muscle of the larger hotel chains won out. Between 1969 and 1978, for example, six hotels were built in and around the historic neighborhood, adding 695 rooms to the city's portfolio.

The sixteen-story Marriott was built in 2004 to a substantial amount of opposition, but the city's planning commission voted 6–1 to allow an exception to the law concerning the height of new buildings. For right or wrong, the economic pressure threatened by disregarding tourist dollars often proved too strong to resist.

The moratorium also drove hotel construction in the CBD, on Canal Street and in the Warehouse District. In 1972, for example, between Chartres Street and Dorsiere Place, an entire block was leveled and a forty-two-story Marriott was erected, instantly becoming the city's tallest and most modern hotel. This also drew anger from the preservationists, one famously calling the Marriott "an oversized plastic riverboat."

NEW ORLEANS HISTORIC HOTELS

An exterior shot of the modern-day Ritz Carlton Hotel.

Other events spurred even more growth. The announcement of the 1984 World's Fair—aka the Louisiana World Exposition—brought the forty-seven-story Sheraton Hotel, as well as the lower-rise Le Meridian on Canal, now the JW Marriott.

By the 1990s, development on Canal had slowed considerably, though some old buildings were appropriated. The larger department stores were dying thanks to a huge middle-class exodus from the city, so plenty of large spaces were up for grabs, perfect for housing all those incoming tourists.

DH Holmes (immortalized in the opening chapters of that great New Orleans novel, *A Confederacy of Dunces*) became the Chateau Sonesta Hotel, which later became the Hyatt French Quarter. In 2001, the famous old Maison Blanche department store was transformed into the huge Ritz Carlton that dominates that stretch of Canal today. The site of the old Marks Isaacs store now makes up part of the Astor Crowne Plaza.

By the early 2000s, mostly due to the three- and four-star additions in the CBD and Warehouse District, room capacity in the city had rocketed to thirty-seven thousand rooms for ten million annual tourists, with numerous historic structures converted into boutique hotels.

Fashionable independents, such as International House, sprang up, as did the trendier brands of international chains. Starwood Hotels brought not

NEW ORLEANS HISTORIC HOTELS

An exterior shot of the modern-day Le Marais Hotel.

one but two W Hotels to the city—the Poydras Street and French Quarter hotels catering to different clienteles.

These mixed with big players offering a more traditional experience. The Windsor Court, for example, is plum next to Harrah's Casino but offers guests the refinement of afternoon tea service and an atmosphere that recalls a centuries-old British institution. The Loews, too, facing the W over Poydras, retains that high-end elegance and traditional service standards. Whereas the W aims for "vibe," the Loews aims for "ambience" (by the time of publishing, the W on Poydras will have become Le Meridien).

The months and years following the summer of 2005 after Hurricane Katrina and the subsequent failure of the federal levee system meant severe closures for downtown hotels. Although sustained devastation was more prevalent in outlying neighborhoods, the damage to downtown properties was substantial, and a number of places closed.

The Ritz-Carlton, the Hyatt Regency and the Fairmont all closed, the shortest period being the fifteen-month closure of the Ritz-Carlton. All these hotels took the opportunity for major refurbishments, complete structural reworking and—in the case of the Fairmont, which reopened as the Roosevelt—rebranding. The Hyatt Regency took six years to be rebuilt and reopen. The Jung Hotel, which was already struggling, closed completely.

During the state of emergency and in the immediate aftermath, hotels acted as shelters, centers for volunteers and aid efforts as well as temporary housing for their own staff. The Monteleone, for example, with typical concern for its employees, took in as many as it could and, according to personal stories, fed people (see the interview with Charlie Farrae in Appendix I).

To stage his press conferences, Mayor Nagin also enlisted the Sheraton, which, as the *New York Times* reported at the time, was "heavily fortified...on Canal Street, a locale thick with clean-up crews and one where beefy private security personnel armed with weapons guarded the single entrance that was open."

The events following the levee failure are obviously a massively involved and complex set of incomparably tragic circumstances. In reducing them to a brief few paragraphs here, I don't mean to trivialize them in any way. There are many books by vastly more qualified writers available should you wish to find out more. I recommend *One Dead in the Attic* by Chris Rose, and *Breach of Faith: Hurricane Katrina and the Near Death of a Great American City*, written by former *Times-Picayune* city editor Jed Horne.

Since the events displaced one million people, New Orleans's recovery was an immediate concern, though it quickly became apparent that—despite being underpopulated—the city would come back. It took a couple of years, but tourism, Mardi Gras crowds, the number of restaurants and the hotel room capacity soon made it back to pre-Katrina levels.

Slightly smaller-scale, boutique-style hotels seem to be the immediate future of New Orleans tourism as it consolidates its place as a year-round destination. Properties such as Le Marais and the Mazarin are modern yet have slipped without too much intrusion into the Old World façade of their French Quarter surroundings. The Hotel Modern at Lee Circle is another quietly fashionable affair. This property was a hotel called Le Cirque for a long time, itself a redevelopment of the residential YMCA, so hospitality in this location is a long-standing business.

The very newest hotels at the time of writing are contrasting properties. The Saint on Canal Street stands in contrast to its Ritz-Carlton neighbor, a markedly brasher affair, touting a more 'rock star' experience. The two new Hyatts—one (Hyatt Regency) a huge convention-friendly beast of a property near the Superdome, the other (Hyatt French Quarter) a more laid back, low-rise affair in the Quarter—are both good-looking, sleek and ultra modern.

An exterior shot of the modern-day Mazarin Hotel.

An exterior shot of the modern-day W French Quarter.

In many ways, these three hotels between them represent the emerging markets of the city—conventions, sophisticated travelers looking for low-key elegance and the out-and-out party crowd. Perhaps these were always the main markets for the city—just swap convention delegates for trades people and Bourbon Street revelers for classical music and ball attendees, and you've got New Orleans in the nineteenth century.

Thinking back to the quote from Lafcadio Hearn that opened this book, I think if he returned today, Hearn would still find hotel life a "centre of gaiety" in New Orleans. Take a drink on almost any night at any of the old bars—a Sazerac at the Roosevelt or a Carousel at the Monteleone—and you'll see.

Businessmen, bachelorette parties, gossiping locals, drinking tourists, off-duty bartenders and decompressing waitstaff, pirates huddled in corners divvying out their booty (OK, this last crowd are probably just on their way to a costume party)—all of New Orleans life is still there in the hotel bars. Reassuringly, there's still the "dash of excitement and Bohemianism" that seduced Lafcadio Hearn so readily, and despite the challenges of New Orleans life, when all's said and done, that really can't be said for too many American cities these days.

Appendix I
MEETING THE OFFICIAL HISTORIAN OF THE HOTEL MONTELEONE

As I arrive at the Monteleone to meet Charlie Farrae, I see him straight away, even though I have no idea what he looks like. He's a burly presence that immediately dominates the hotel lobby, charismatic even from a distance and happily chatting away to an elderly woman.

I wait as they finish up. "Who was that?" I ask as we introduce ourselves and shake hands. "Oh, she was born in the building next door to the hotel and just passes through three or four times a week to say hello," Charlie says, matter of fact like—nothing unusual there for him.

We find seats in the hotel's famous Carousel Bar. It's late morning, and the bar is pretty empty; the bartenders are slicing fruit and stocking ice. "This place used to be a supper club," Charlie comments. "It was so popular and so small that you couldn't get in if you didn't get there early." Pleasantries over, Charlie gets straight into it.

"I've been here forty-six years. People stay and work at this hotel a long time because they treat you well. There's a bellboy that was here for fifty-two years, a maintenance guy was here for fifty, a waitress for fifty-three years. Let me tell you this, a guy called Johnny was the food and beverage manager and the owner paid off his mortgage just because he felt like doing a kind deed."

This is Charlie Farrae's opening gambit—it's more amiable and less defensive than it sounds, but Charlie really loves the Hotel Monteleone and what it stands for. He's an old-school hotel guy, probably glad to be coming to the end of his career around now, when old-school hotel stuff like paying

APPENDIX I

off a guy's mortgage doesn't happen so often. Corporations are involved. Shareholders. You can't just slip Johnny a few thousand bucks and call it a nice gesture. More's the pity.

Charlie started his hotel career at the place across the road. "I worked at the Roosevelt for fifteen years," he says. "I left there on a Wednesday and started at the Monteleone on the very next day."

He gave more effusive praise for the old ways, for the days when management had a personal relationship with long-term employees to the point of getting involved in their lives. "My daughter wanted her wedding reception at the hotel," he says. "I went to the boss, and he gave it to me for cost. I was so pleased I did this with all three of my daughters *and* one of my granddaughters. Employees often borrowed money from the hotel and paid it back as they liked, without interest. This was in the days before credit unions, of course."

Charlie has seen a lot of firsts in his time. "We were the first hotel to be air-conditioned," he says, laughing. "First we put it in the lobby, then one room on each floor until it got popular. The management [was] reticent, though; 'People will get pneumonia, and we'll get sued!' said the GM."

"We used to rent TVs out at a dollar a day. When we finally put them in the rooms, we put black-and-white sets in the cheaper rooms, and only the more expensive rooms and suites had color sets."

He strays into nostalgia as he thinks about the times before all people wanted was free Wi-Fi. "Bourbon Street was all piano bars and jazz. People wore suits to go out on Bourbon Street. Hard to imagine that now." We glance out the window, me nodding as if I was in any position to know any different.

I ask him about the big New Orleans occasions. What was the place like around Mardi Gras? "Some of the parades passed down Royal Street, and since we had a balcony, we were a very popular destination. To be honest, room was at such a premium that it was always a big headache for me, knowing who to give tickets to. Everyone wanted them. People would get very jealous."

"We had Elvis here when he was starting out. Talk about a nice boy. They came to register—[he] and his cousin strode into the lobby looking like they just got off a motorcycle. But he was a nice boy. We had them all: Bob Hope, Bing Crosby, Tyrone Power, John Wayne, Jimmy Stewart. Tyrone Power was supposed to get a large suite, and we'd given him a slightly smaller one. He came down to the desk on the day he arrived, and he wasn't too happy. 'I'm going to rehearsal, and when I get back I want a

APPENDIX I

larger suite. I'm not spending another night in that cubby hole.' I believe we accommodated him."

Charlie helped the stars in other ways, too, though. "Jon Voight was here trying to pick up the local dialect for some film or other. Everyone thinks I'm from New York, and a lot of local people here sound like they're from Brooklyn. I told him he had to get out into Cajun country—the people sound very different out there.

"When [Joe] Frazier came to New Orleans to fight, we put a ring up on the roof and charged people three dollars to go and watch him spar. I was given fifty-dollar tickets to go and see the fight, but I couldn't go. The owner took them off my hands and said he would just go and sell them at the gate—the owner of the hotel scalping tickets! It happened the same way with the Superbowl one year. My daughter needed tickets, and the owner said they had two to spare and gave them to her."

For Charlie, though, the everyday people provide as many good memories as the celebrities. He tells me a touching story about the mother of one of his regular hotel guests. "One day a woman comes in with her sons ashes. He was a regular here and loved the hotel. She wanted to put some in the pot that the flowers in the lobby stood in…

"You're with good people all the time. You get to know your colleagues and the guests that come back year after year. They become like old friends. I'm now taking care of the grandchildren of all kinds of people that came here years and years ago. You forge relationships that last…

"After Katrina we were closed from August to October, but we all got paid in full. The owner said we could stay here if we needed to. Billy made every pay check out for a little extra. He said, 'We need you more than you need us.' He fed his employees. He did everything he could for them."

Charlie is steadfast in his praise for the hotel, and you can tell it isn't just a PR spin to make the place look good. He's emotional about this place. "I'm not going to quit. I'd be dead in six months. I have three days off as it is, and I get depressed. I was working here six to seven days a week, 8:00 a.m. to 10:00 p.m. I did it all. I saw it all."

And with that we shake hands and wander back to the lobby, and as he walks through, there's a chorus of "Hey there, mister Charlie" from almost everyone he passes.

Appendix II
RECIPES FROM SELECTED NEW ORLEANS HOTELS

The Peychaud Sazerac Cocktail

The cocktail is most associated with the Roosevelt Hotel, of course, which after all has its bar named for the drink. However, without the influence of one of Maison de Ville's most famous residents, it wouldn't exist in its best-loved form.

1 cube sugar
1½ ounces Sazerac rye whiskey or Buffalo Trace bourbon
¼ ounce Herbsaint/absinthe
3 dashes Peychaud's bitters
lemon peel

Pack an old-fashioned glass with ice. In a second old-fashioned glass, place the sugar cube and add the Peychaud's bitters to it. Then crush the sugar cube. Add the Sazerac rye whiskey or Buffalo Trace bourbon to the second glass containing the Peychaud's bitters and sugar. Empty the ice from the first glass and coat the glass with the Herbsaint/absinthe. Discard the remaining Herbsaint/absinthe. Empty the whiskey/bitters/sugar mixture from the second glass into the first glass and garnish with lemon peel.

APPENDIX II

The Ramos Gin Fizz

This recipe and the rights to this cocktail were acquired from Ramos himself by the Roosevelt Hotel.

2 ounces gin (London Dry or Old Tom)
1 ounce heavy cream
1 ounce simple syrup
½ ounce fresh-squeezed lemon juice
½ ounce fresh-squeezed lime juice
1 egg white
3 dashes orange blossom water
1 drop vanilla extract (optional)

Combine the ingredients in a shaker and dry shake (without ice) for two minutes. Add several ice cubes and shake hard for several minutes. Continue shaking for as long as you can, at least until you can no longer hear the ice inside. Pour the contents into a chilled Collins glass and slowly top with soda water to make a frothy head. A straw is optional, but the mixture should be so thick that the straw would stand on its own in the center of the drink.

Hurricane

A classic New Orleans cocktail, this is the JW Marriot's own version.

1½ ounces Bacardi light rum
1½ ounces Meyers Dark Rum
½ ounce pomegranate liqueur (such as Pama)
¼ ounce lemon juice
¼ ounce lime juice
¼ ounce simple syrup
¼ ounce grenadine
2 ounces pineapple juice
1 cherry, for garnish

Shake all the ingredients, except the dark rum, with ice. Pour and then top with the dark rum. Garnish with a cherry.

APPENDIX II

Vieux Carré Cocktail

In 1938, during the height of the Great Depression, head bartender at the Hotel Monteleone, Walter Bergeron, introduced the Vieux Carré Cocktail at what was then the Swan Bar. It was created as a tribute to the ethnic groups of the city: the bénédictine and cognac to the French influence, Sazerac rye as a tribute to the American influence, sweet Vermouth to the Italian influence and the bitters as a tribute to the Caribbean's. Prohibition had been lifted only a few years earlier as a way of stimulating commerce. Bergeron's Vieux Carré Cocktail was successful in bringing visitors to the hotel bar and remains a favorite today.

¼ ounce bénédictine
¼ ounce cognac
½ ounce Sazerac rye
¼ ounce sweet vermouth
3 drops Angostura bitters
3 drops Peychaud's bitters
lemon twist

Pour ingredients over ice in an eight-ounce rocks glass, stir well and garnish with a lemon twist.

Polo Martini

From the Polo Lounge of the Windsor Court Hotel comes this take on the classic martini.

2 ounces Stolichnaya vodka or Bombay Sapphire
2 ounces Perrier Jouet Champagne
3 drops of Peychaud's bitters

Mix drink in a lipped snifter glass. Combine above ingredients in the snifter with ice. To garnish, spear separately olives, onions and lemon peel twists. Place in a silver finger bowl. To serve table side, pour the mixture from the lipped snifter into a chilled martini glass and offer garnish.

APPENDIX II

Queso Fundido al Tequila

A recipe that, while not typically New Orleans in nature, comes from the owners of the Maison de Ville.

1 tablespoon extra virgin olive oil
2 medium tomatoes, cut into ¼-inch dice
2 jalapeño peppers, seeded and minced
1 small onion, cut into ¼-inch dice
kosher salt
3 tablespoons Dos Lunas tequila
½ pound Monterey Jack cheese, shredded
coarsely chopped cilantro, to taste
warm corn tortillas or tortilla chips for serving

In a large skillet, heat the olive oil. Add the tomatoes, jalapeños, onion and a large pinch of salt and cook over a medium-high heat, stirring often, until softened. Pour in the tequila and cook, stirring frequently, until the skillet looks nearly dry (about 2 minutes). Reduce the heat to low. Add the cheese and cook stirring constantly until fully melted (about 1 minute). Quickly transfer to a serving bowl. Sprinkle with cilantro and serve immediately with tortillas or chips.

Blue Crab Gratin

This recipe comes from the Grill Room at the Windsor Court Hotel.

3 large shallots, sliced
3 cloves garlic, sliced
1 cup sherry
1 quart heavy cream
18 stalks asparagus
5 red radishes
½ cup white wine vinegar
3 cloves black garlic
1 pound jumbo lump blue crab
6 teaspoons paddlefish caviar

APPENDIX II

1 ounce manchego cheese, grated
salt and pepper, to taste
6 slices manchego cheese (sliced across the diameter of the wheel)

For the Sherry Cream

In a medium sauce pan, gently sauté shallots and garlic until translucent. Add sherry and reduce over medium heat until sherry is nearly evaporated and mixture is syrupy. Add half of the heavy cream and bring to a boil. Remove from heat and cover. Allow to steep at room temperature for 30 minutes. Strain and cool completely.

For the Garnish

Remove the stem from the asparagus to make 1-inch spears, reserving the stems for another use. Remove the stem and root end of the radishes. Cut each radish into four pieces. In a small sauté pan, combine asparagus, radishes and vinegar and cook over medium-high heat until vinegar is nearly evaporated. Add ½ cup of water to the pan and repeat process. When the water is nearly gone, taste a piece of radish. It should be tender. If not, add more water and continue to cook until tender. Peel the black garlic and slice each clove into three slivers.

To Finish

Pick crab over to remove shells. Bring the remaining cream to a boil in a medium pot. Add crab, caviar and grated manchego. Stir thoroughly. Continue to cook until the mixture is shiny and has large bubbles. Season with salt and pepper. Divide mixture into six small wide-rimmed bowls. Top each with three asparagus tips, three braised radishes and three slivers of black garlic. Lay a slice of manchego over the mixture. Under a grill, or using a blowtorch, brown each until the cheese is translucent and golden brown. Serves 6.

Appendix III
HISTORICAL GUIDEBOOK HOTEL DIRECTORIES

These are excerpts from the original books:

1. Lafcadio Hearn, 1885:
Historical Sketch Book and Guide to New Orleans and Environs

There are besides the St. Charles and the Hotel Royale, a number of other hotels in New Orleans, as follows:

Cassidy's, 174 Gravier.
City Hotel, Camp, corner of Common.
Hotel Chalmette, 98 St. Charles.
Hotel Vonderbanck, 40 to 46 Magazine.
Waverley House, Poydras, corner of Camp.

The boarding houses of New Orleans are too numerous to mention, amounting to several hundred, from the very cheapest lodging-house to the finest establishments whose prices exceed those of the hotels.

APPENDIX III

2. JAMES S. ZACHARIE, 1902:
NEW ORLEANS GUIDE, WITH DESCRIPTIONS OF THE ROUTES TO NEW ORLEANS

The city has, during the last few years, made great progress. New modern hotels have been erected and sky-scraping office buildings have been built. Many streets have been asphalted and repaved with a Rosetta gravel that concretes naturally, and thus whole quarters of the city have been improved.

New St. Charles Hotel, No. 215 St. Charles Street. One square from Canal street. 465 rooms. Elevators. American plan: $3.50 and up. European plan: Rooms $1.50 and up.

Hotel Grunewald, No. 120 Baronne Street, near Canal Street. 320 rooms. Elevators. European plan: Rooms $1.00 and up.

Cosmopolitan Hotel, No. 128 Bourbon Street, near Canal Street. 125 rooms. Elevator. European plan: Rooms $1.50 and up.

Commercial Hotel, No. 204 Royal Street, corner Customhouse street, one square from Canal street. 170 rooms. Elevator. European plan: Rooms $1.00 and up, bath included.

Hotel Denechaud, No. 348 Carondelet Street, four squares from Canal street. 100 rooms. Elevator. American plan: $2.00 per day and up; European plan: Rooms $1.00 and up. French cuisine.

Hotel de Louisiane, No. 717 Customhouse street, one square from Canal Street. 50 rooms. (In the old Zacharie mansion.) Celebrated for its fine French and Creole cuisine. European plan: Rooms 50 cents and up, bath included.

Park View Hotel, No. 618 Camp Street, opposite Lafayette Square, five squares from Canal Street. 50 rooms. Elevator. American plan: $1.00 and up; European plan: Rooms 50 cents and up, bath included.

St. Charles Mansion, No. 826 St. Charles Street. 50 rooms. European plan: Rooms $1.00 and up.

Fabacher's Hotel, No. 709 Customhouse Street. European plan: Rooms 75 cents and up, including bath.

Extracts

Shrove Monday. This day, called by the French Lundi Gras, is celebrated by the reception of the King of the Carnival. His Majesty (called "Rex") arrives in state at the foot of Canal street and, escorted by the military and the Dukes of his realm, visits the City Hall, where the keys of the city are presented

APPENDIX III

to him by the Mayor. The King then goes to the St. Charles Hotel and holds a reception. In the evening, His Majesty, attended by a brilliant suite, visits the theatres in state. The entrance of the King and his court into the royal state box is heralded by the orchestra playing the royal anthem. Also, on this evening, the ball of the Knights of Proteus, with a street pageant, takes place, followed by a ball at one of the theatres.

Passing down Chartres street, among dilapidated houses and hotels, the wrecks of former times, Toulouse street is reached.

3. *New Orleans City Guide*, 1938

Although New Orleans normally possesses ample hotel and other facilities for the many thousands who come yearly to enjoy its mild climate, romantic atmosphere, Mid-Winter Sports Carnival, and world famed Mardi Gras, to prevent possible inconvenience or disappointment it is suggested that visitors write or wire in advance for accommodations desired, especially during the winter months.

DeSoto Hotel, 420 Baronne St.; 226 rooms all with hot and cold running water, and 175 with private bath; rates $1.50 up, European plan; garage 50c extra; convention hall, writing-room, restaurant (lunch 60c, dinner $1), coffee shop, and bar.

Jung Hotel, 1500 Canal St.; 700 rooms, all with private bath, running ice water, ceiling fans, servidor, and outside exposure; rates $3–$4, European plan; parking lot 15c extra; roof garden, three convention halls, dining-room, coffee shop, bar, Turkish baths, barber shop, and beauty parlor.

Lafayette Hotel, 628 St. Charles St.; 80 rooms, all with running water and ceiling fans 55 with private baths; rates, $1.75 up, European plan; garage 50c extra.

LaSalle Hotel, 1113 Canal St.; 100 rooms 70 with ceiling fans, and 50 with private bath; rates, $1.25–$2.50, European plan; garage 50c extra.

Monteleone Hotel, 214 Royal St.; 600 rooms 540 have radios, 500 have private baths, and all have hot and cold running water and ceiling fans; rates $1.50–$3.50. European plan; garage 50c, parking lot 15c; convention hall, dining-room, coffee shop, bar, and beauty parlor.

New Orleans Hotel, 1300 Canal St.; 275 rooms, all with private bath and ceiling fan; rates $3 up, European plan; garage 50f extra; convention hall, air-conditioned dining-room and coffee shop, writing-room, and barber shop.

APPENDIX III

Roosevelt Hotel, 123 Baronne St.; 700 rooms, 400 air-conditioned; rates $3.50 up. European plan; garage 50c extra; convention halls, dining rooms, coffee shop, bar, cocktail lounge, beauty parlor, Turkish baths, etc.

Senator Hotel, 208 Dauphine St.; 115 rooms 68 with private baths; rates $1 up.

St. Charles Hotel, 211 St. Charles St.; 600 rooms with hot and cold water, and radio all with private bath; rates $3 up; European plan; dining room, bar, barber shop, beauty parlor, writing-rooms, etc.

Appendix IV
NEW ORLEANS HISTORIC HOTEL DIRECTORY

The historic hotels in this list are still in business today.

Andrew Jackson Hotel
919 Royal Street, (504) 561-5881, frenchquarterinns.com/andrewjackson

Audubon Cottages
509 Dauphine Street, (504) 586-1516, auduboncottages.com

Bienville House
320 Decatur Street, (504) 529-2345, bienvillehouse.com

Bourbon Orleans
717 Orleans Street, (504) 523-2222, bourbonorleans.com

The Cornstalk Hotel
915 Royal Street, (504) 523-1515, cornstalkhotel.com

Dauphine Orleans
415 Dauphine Street, (504) 586-1800, dauphineorleans.com

Hotel Monteleone
214 Royal Street, (504) 523-3341, hotelmonteleone.com

APPENDIX IV

Hotel Provincial
1024 Chartres Street, (504) 581-4995, hotelprovincial.com

Lafitte Guest House
1003 Bourbon Street, (504) 581-2678, laffiteguesthouse.com

Le Pavillon
833 Poydras Street, (800) 535-9095, lepavillon.com

Le Richelieu
1234 Chartres Street, (504) 529-2492, lerichelieuhotel.com

Maison de Ville
727 Toulouse Street, (504) 324-4888, maisondeville.com

Omni Royal Orleans
621 St. Louis Street, (504) 529-5333, omnihotels.com

Place D'Armes
625 St. Ann Street, (888) 626-5917, placedarmes.com

The Roosevelt New Orleans Hotel
130 Roosevelt Way, (800) 925-3673, therooseveltneworleans.com

Soniat House
1133 Chartres Street, (504) 522-0570, soniathouse.com

BIBLIOGRAPHY

Adams, Jenny. *The Hotel Monteleone: More Than a Landmark, the Heart of New Orleans since 1886*. New Orleans, LA: Hotel Monteleone, 2011. (www.jennyadamsfreelance.com).
Arthur, Stanley. *Old New Orleans: A History of the Vieux Carré, Its Ancient and Historical Buildings*. Gretna, LA: Pelican Publishing, 1936.
Asbury, Herbert. *The French Quarter: An Informal History of the NO Underworld*. New York: Knopf, 1936.
Asher, Sally. *Weathering a Dry Spell*. www.sallyasher.com, 2014.
Buckingham, James Silk. *The Slave States of America*. London, UK: Fisher, 1842.
Campanella, Richard. *Bienville's Dilemma*. Lafayette, LA: University of Louisiana at Lafayette Press, 2008.
Castellanos, Henry C. *New Orleans as It Was*. New Orleans, LA: L. Graham, 1895.
Christovich, Mary Louise. *New Orleans Architecture*. Vol. 2, *The American Sector*. Gretna, LA: Pelican Publishing, 1998.
DeMers, John. *French Quarter Royalty: The Tumultuous Life and Times of the Omni Royal Hotel*. New Orleans, LA: Omni Royal Hotel, 1993.
Federal Writers' Project. *New Orleans City Guide*. Federal Writers' Project of the Works Administration, 1938.
Galsworthy, John. *The Inn of Tranquility*. From essays published in the *Fortnightly Review*, 1912.
Hearn, Lafcadio: *Historical Sketch Book and Guide to New Orleans and Environs, with Map: Illustrated with Many Original Engravings, and Containing Exhaustive

BIBLIOGRAPHY

Accounts of the Traditions, Historical Legends, and Remarkable Localities of the Creole City. New York: W.H. Coleman, 1885.

Hémard, Ned. *New Orleans Nostalgia, Remembering New Orleans History, Culture and Traditions*. www.neworleansbar.org.

Horne, Jed. *Breach of Faith: Hurricane Katrina and the Near Death of a Great American City*. New York: Random House, 2008.

Kendall, John. *History of New Orleans*. General Books, LLC, 1922.

Latrobe, Benjamin. *The Journal of Latrobe*. New York: Appleton, 1905.

Martin, François Xavier. *The History of Louisiana from the Earliest Period*. New Orleans, LA: A.T. Penniman, 1827.

Reeves, William D. *Le Pavillon Hotel, A Century of Triumph*. New Orleans, LA: Le Pavillon Hotel, 2008.

Ripley, Eliza. *Social Life in Old New Orleans, Being Recollections of my Girlhood*. New York: Ripley, 1912.

Rose, Chris. *One Dead in the Attic*. New York: Simon and Schuster, 2007.

Starr, S. Fredrick. *Inventing New Orleans: Writings of Lafcadio Hearn*. Jackson: University Press of Mississippi, 2001.

Widmer, Mary Lou. *New Orleans in the Twenties*. Gretna, LA: Pelican Publishing, 1993.

Wiltz, Christine. *The Last Madam: A Life in the New Orleans Underground*. Cambridge, MA: Da Capo Press, 2001.

Wortley, Lady Emmeline Stuart. *Travels Within the United States During 1849 and 1850*. London: Richard Bently, 1851.

Zacharie, James S. *New Orleans Guide, with Descriptions of the Routes to New Orleans, Sights of the City Arranged Alphabetically*. New Orleans, LA, 1902.

ABOUT THE AUTHOR

Paul Oswell is a writer and travel journalist. He was born in Chorley, Lancashire, England. He has written for a wide variety of national newspapers and magazines since 1999, reporting from all seven continents (yes, including Antarctica). He has been based in New Orleans since 2011 and has been visiting the city since 2001. He has edited several guidebooks to the city, including work for Fodor's and Dorling Kindersley, and he is the author of the guide *New Orleans for Free* (2014). You can find out more and contact him via his website: www.pauloswell.com.

Visit us at
www.historypress.net

This title is also available as an e-book

www.ingramcontent.com/pod-product-compliance
Lightning Source LLC
Chambersburg PA
CBHW042142160426
43201CB00022B/2379